STRESS AND PRODUCTIVITY

STRESS AND PRODUCTIVITY

Edited by

Leonard W. Krinsky, Ph.D.
South Oaks Hospital
Amityville, New York

Sherman N. Kieffer, M.D.
State University of New York at Stony Brook
Stony Brook, New York

Pasquale A. Carone, M.D.
South Oaks Hospital
Amityville, New York

Stanley F. Yolles, M.D.
State University of New York at Stony Brook
Stony Brook, New York

Volume IX in the Series
Problems of Industrial Psychiatric Medicine

Series Editor: Sherman N. Kieffer, M.D.

 **HUMAN SCIENCES PRESS, INC.**
72 FIFTH AVENUE
NEW YORK, N.Y. 10011

Library of Congress Cataloging in Publication Data
Main entry under title:

Stress and productivity.

(Problems of industrial psychiatric medicine; v. 9)
Papers of a conference held Apr. 2–3, 1981, at South Oaks Hospital,
Amityville, N.Y., sponsored by South Oaks Foundation and the Dept. of
Psychiatry, State University of New York at Stony Brook.
Bibliography, p.
Includes index.
1. Job stresses—Congresses. I. Krinksy, Leonard W. II. South Oaks
Foundation. III. State University of New York at Stony Brook. Dept. of
Psychiatry.

IV. Series. [DNLM: 1. Stress, Psychological—Congresses. 2. Efficiency—
Congresses. W1 PR574M v. 9 / WM 172 S9133 1981]
HF5548.85.S745 1984   158.7   83-22606
ISBN 0-89885-137-8
ISSN 0277-4178

CONTENTS

Contributors   v

Preface   ix

Introduction   xi

Acknowledgments   xiii

1. **WORK STRESS—A PSYCHIATRIC FRAME OF REFERENCE**   1
   Alan A. McLean, M.D.
   DISCUSSION   14

2. **MANAGING STRESS**   15
   Leon J. Warshaw, M.D.
   DISCUSSION   30

3. **LABOR LOOKS AT WORK STRESS**   55
   Melvin A. Glasser
   DISCUSSION   65

4. **SOCIO-CULTURAL ASPECTS OF STRESS**   80
   Harold M. Visotsky, M.D.
   DISCUSSION   92

5. **STRESS—HOW USEFUL A CONCEPT?**   111
   Joseph N. Ruocco, Ph.D.
   DISCUSSION   121

6. **MEDICAL MANAGEMENT OF STRESS**   141
   Stephen D. Shappell, M.D.
   DISCUSSION   153

Index   174

CONTRIBUTORS

LEONARD S. BRAHEN, PH. D., M.D.
Medical Director
Nassau County Department of Drug and Alcohol Addiction

ROSEMARIE CARLSON, PH.D.
Staff Psychologist
South Oaks Hospital

PATRICK F. CARONE, M.D., M.P.H.
Assistant Director
Professional Education
South Oaks Hospital

FRED B. CHARATAN, M.D.
Chief of Psychiatry
Jewish Institute of Geriatric Care
Long Island Jewish-Hillside Medical Center

THOMAS CONLEY
Personnel Relations
Grumman Aerospace Corporation

JOHN J. DOWLING, M.D., M.P.H.
Commissioner
Nassau County Department of Health

VINCENT GALLAGHER, M.D.
Medical Department
Grumman Aerospace Corporation

MELVIN A. GLASSER, ESQ.
Consultant
International Union
United Auto Workers

MAURICE GOLDENHAR, M.D.
Associate Professor of Family Medicine
School of Medicine
State University of New York at Stony Brook

IRVING HAMMERSCHLAG, M.D.
Medical Director
Long Island Lighting Company

DAVID HARRIS, M.D., M.P.H.
Commissioner
Suffolk County Department of Health Services

AUDREY H. JONES
Personnel Policies and Services Manager
Long Island Lighting Company

GOTTFRIED F. H. LEHMANN, M.D., M.A.
Medical Director
Chief Medical Officer
Long Island Rail Road

ALBERT T. LOJKO, M.D.
New York Area Medical Director
Trans World Airlines

ROSEMARY LUKTON, D.S.W.
Professor
School of Social Work
Adelphi University

ALAN A. McLEAN, M.D.
Eastern Area Medical Director
IBM

Clinical Associate Professor of Psychiatry
Cornell University Medical College

EDMUND C. NEUHAUS, PH.D.
Executive Director
The Rehabilitation Institute

RAUL PAEZ, M.D.
Senior Psychiatrist
South Oaks Hospital

BARTON PAKULL, M.D.
Acting Chief
Office of Aviation Medicine
Department of Transportation
Federal Aviation Administration

MICHAEL J. PETRIZZI, C.S.W.
Director
Nassau County Administration
Diocese of Rockville Centre
Catholic Charities

JOSEPH N. RUOCCO, PH.D.
Industrial Psychologist
President
J.N. Ruocco Associates

MAURICE S. SATIN, PH.D.
Assistant Director
Division of Mental Health Care Systems
Long Island Research Institute
New York State Office of Mental Health

JULIAN H. SCHWARTZ, M.D.
Consultant in Internal Medicine
South Oaks Hospital

ISIDORE SHAPIRO, A.C.S.W.
Commissioner
Nassau County Department of Mental Health

STEPHEN D. SHAPPELL, M.D.
Clinical Associate Professor of Medicine
Cornell University Medical College

Consulting Cardiologist
South Oaks Hospital

ARTHUR A. STONE, PH.D.
Research Scientist
Long Island Research Institute
State University of New York at Stony Brook

PETER VAN PUTTEN, JR.
Director of Personnel
Hazeltine Corporation

HAROLD M. VISOTSKY, M.D.
Owen L. Coon Professor of Psychiatry
Chairman
Department of Psychiatry and Behavioral Sciences
Northwestern University Medical School

Director
Institute of Psychiatry
Northwestern Memorial Hospital

LEON J. WARSHAW, M.D.
Executive Director
New York Business Group on Health

CHARLES WINICK
Consultant
Central Labor Rehabilitation Council of New York, Inc.

PREFACE

In 1971, South Oaks Foundation sponsored the first of what has come to be a yearly conference relating to problems in industrial psychiatric medicine. A year later the Department of Psychiatry, Health Sciences Center, State University of New York at Stony Brook, joined in collaborative efforts with the South Oaks Foundation in sponsoring yearly conferences. These conferences provide a forum wherein representatives of psychiatry, psychology and social work meet in collaborative efforts with representatives of labor, management and government. This volume, Stress and Productivity, is the ninth one relating to problems of industrial psychiatric medicine.

The first conference was in 1971 and was entitled "Alcoholism in Industry." Since that time, South Oaks Foundation and the Department of Psychiatry of the Medical School at Stony Brook have involved themselves with topics such as Drug Abuse in Industry, Women in Industry, Misfits in Industry, A Look at the Aging Employee.

This volume comes out of a conference entitled "Stress and Productivity" which took place on April 2 and 3, 1981 at South Oaks Hospital, Amityville, New York. It addressed the concept of stress as it affects the employee, employer and the workplace. It examined the effects of debilitating stress and what it does to previously efficient and dedicated workers. The employer's role in the management and alleviation of stress is a very important part of this book, as are lengthy discussions as to when professional help is appropriate.

In this book a synthesis of opinions was sought from those with varying viewpoints. Certain problems are inherently incapable of solution, but there are many other areas where representatives of various diverse groups can work together to establish a common denominator. This is the purpose of these meetings and the book that comes from them.

INTRODUCTION

"Stress" is a part of everyday life and may well have a positive
energizing effect. It is overwhelming or poorly managed stress
which can cause a staggering array of psychological, physiological and sociological problems." Welcoming remarks, Pas-
quale A. Carone, M.D., Chairman

What is stress? One definition says it is the product of the
interaction between individuals and their environmental expectations. Another definition is that stress is a state of bodily or
mental tension resulting from factors that tend to alter an existing
equilibrium. In many ways, stress is like a violin string. If the
string is pulled too tight, it snaps; if it is too slack, it doesn't make
music.

We know that stress is a part of everyday life for everyone.
In fact, a certain amount of stress can, and does, have a positive,
energizing effect. But overwhelming stress or poorly managed
stress can cause a staggering array of psychological, physiological,
and sociological problems. Headaches, hypertension, back pain,
irritability, apathy, depression, alcoholism, job loss, marital
problems . . . the list can go on and on.

This book is concerned with bringing together members of
various disciplines to address the problems of stress as they affect
the employee, employer and the work place. It is our hope that
by having representatives of the mental health professions meet
with representatives of labor and management, we can mean-
ingfully face a problem that is present and will continue to grow
in importance. We must examine the role of the employer when
an employee's level of productivity is greatly reduced by poorly
managed stress. We must look at the effects on the worker and
the worker's family. The socio-cultural aspects of stress are a
most important consideration and the medical management of
stress is an ever-present concern. The role of the mental health
disciplines in anticipating stress situations, in being able to help

people meet the devastating effects of stress, have to be taken into account.

This conference brought together these representatives of various diverse and yet interrelated disciplines. The conclusions are clear. The psychological, physiological and financial aspects of stress are devastating. It is our hope that the conference and the book that came from it will provide a greater understanding of the problem.

ACKNOWLEDGMENTS

The preparation of this volume required not only a great deal of effort on the part of the editors, but very active involvement and cooperation from a number of different groups. Each of the speakers and panelists was contacted on several occasions. It was necessary that they aid us with the editing, which required working with typescripts to further clarify and at times expand on some of their statements at the conference.

The Board of Directors of South Oaks Hospital (The Long Island Home, Ltd.) have actively supported the South Oaks Foundation over the years. They have been particularly interested in the annual industrial psychiatric medicine conferences which are now in their eleventh year. We are deeply indebted to them for their support in working with various problems of psychiatric medicine.

Our acknowledgments would be incomplete without mentioning the tremendous support and cooperation we receive from our executive assistant, Catherine Martens, and our director of public relations, Lynn Black.

Chapter 1

WORK STRESS — A PSYCHIATRIC FRAME OF REFERENCE

Alan A. McLean, M.D.*

*Alan McLean, M.D., is Eastern Area Medical Director for IBM. At Cornell University Medical College he is a Clinical Associate Professor of Psychiatry and an Associate Attending Physician at New York Hospital. Dr. McLean is a Fellow of the American Occupational Medical Association and was its President in 1978 and 1979. He is also a Fellow of the American Academy of Occupational Medicine and a member of the World Health Organizations's Expert Advisory Panel on Occupational Health. He is a member of the New York County and State Medical Societies, the American Medical Association (where he was an Alternate in the House of Delegates), and the Permanent Commission and International Association on Occupational Health. He is a Fellow of the American Psychiatric Association and served for four years as Chair of its Committee on Occupational Psychiatry. He currently serves on the APA Committee on Confidentiality. He is a Diplomate of the American Board of Psychiatry and Neurology and is Board eligible in occupational medicine. In addition to 50 articles in professional journals and textbooks, Dr. McLean is author or co-author of eight books, the latest of which is *Work Stress* (Addison-Wesley). He also edits the Addison-Wesley Series on Occupational Stress.

Over the years, the changing nature and meaning of work have caused more continued restructuring of American lives than any force in our history.

For many reasons, work is a vital process in coping with life's stresses. Work is often the primary means by which a person feels useful in life and establishes significance and personal identity.

Another point: Work is often a form of coping and a refuge. Consider, for example, how people in grief regard work. Many report that, in the process of mourning and reorienting their lives after a major loss, work is not a burden but the best refuge against constant high levels of distress and depression. One speaks here, of course, of "burying one's self in one's work." Thus, work may provide a psychological haven against problems, loneliness, or depression, that otherwise would be insurmountable. For such people, *not* to work is to be deprived of the only viable means of coping with non-work-related stress.

Another consideration comes from Eric Fromm, who said, "Since modern man experiences himself both as a seller and as the commodity to be sold on the market, his self-esteem depends upon conditions beyond his control. If he is successful, he is valuable. If he is not, he is worthless."

Finally from Elliott Jaques, the British psychoanalyst who has done a lot of research in the world of work:

> Working for a living is one of the basic activities in a man's life. By forcing him to come to grips with his environment, with his livelihood at stake, it confronts him with the actuality of his personal capacity to exercise judgment, to achieve concrete and specific results. It gives him a continuous account of his correspondence between outside reality and the inner perception of that reality, as well as an account of the accuracy of his appraisal of himself. In short, a man's work does not satisfy his material needs alone.

So much for a frame of reference. Now to our topic, work stress.

It strikes me that scientific concepts, particularly in the medical and the behavioral areas, lend themselves to some strange and very wonderful uses. For example, I suspect that Sigmund Freud would be quite amazed to see promises to "prevent illness, boost motivation, increase productivity, create conditions favorable to learning and personal growth, (and) reduce strain and anxiety and boredom on the job," by reading a mail-order book on the management of stress.

Work stress has become a topic of considerable currency in both the lay and professional press. In the past several months there have been dozens of books and thousands of articles in publications ranging from the *National Enquirer* to *The New England Journal of Medicine*. My mail, and I am sure much of yours, is laden with brochures describing stress-management conferences, lectures and seminars. I might add, I have rarely seen so many instant experts in my life. Stress, and particularly work stress, is "in." Many of these offerings contain an extraordinarily high percentage of nonsense. Stress is *not* the sole cause of cancer. Stress management programs will *not* prevent major psychiatric illness. So, I urge you to read with skepticism much of the material you see on the topic.

There are some very good and very sound studies in the professional literature, but many of these even sound studies have follow-up reports in the news media that have a tendency at times to present scientific speculation as actual theory, which is not the case. That there is some correlation between stress-related diseases and jobs such as laboring and secretarial work — and there is — does not mean that all or even most laborers or most secretaries work under a heavy load of job-related stress.

I am not here to give you spoon-fed advice. But there are a couple of things one can do to help cope with stressors on the job in a very cognitive way.

I would like to give you two illustrations. The first has to do with a young man, valedictorian of his class, who could have had a scholarship to almost any university in the country, but whose single goal in life when he graduated was to be the best supermarket checkout clerk in town.

He applied to the largest supermarket and was accepted. He did an outstanding job coping with a tremendous amount of occupational stress. For example, a man came in and said, "I want to buy a half a head of cabbage." "But sir," said the young man, "we don't sell cabbage by the half head." The man became irate. Finally the clerk went to the back of the store and talked to his manager. "There is some S.O.B. who wants to buy a half a head of cabbage," and with that he looked over his shoulder— there was the irate customer. "And *this* gentleman wants to buy the other half."

After several months, the manager called him to one side and said, "Look, you have too much talent to be simply a clerk. I want you to go to management school." The clerk thought for a minute and said, "No, I don't want to go to management school, besides it is in Louisville. You know that in Louisville all they have are basketball players and ladies of the night." The manager responded by saying, "Well, my wife is from Louisville." "And what position did she play?"

Coping with stressful situations with mental agility is one thing many of us do and perhaps can do better.

There is another cognitive way one can cope with such stressors. This comes to me from Dr. Ralph Siu who held a number of significant jobs in the Federal government before he retired to be a consultant in social strategy. Several fascinating books are out by Dr. Siu, one is called *The Craft of Power*, which is Machiavelli updated. *The Master Manager* is another and *Transcending the Power Game* is the most recent. They provide fascinating management philosophy.

Ralph's comment is that there is only one thing one needs in order to master work stress and that is, very simply, to learn to play Chinese baseball. Very simple. Well, Chinese baseball is exactly like American baseball: same number of players, same number of bases. There is only one difference: when the ball leaves the pitcher's hand, and as long as that ball is in the air, anyone can move any of the bases anywhere. Mind you, this is coming from a thoughtful, managerial philosopher type who wrote an earlier book called *Tao of Science*.

He is saying, in effect, everything is continually changing — not only events themselves but the very rules governing the judgments that effect those events.

The secret, then, of Chinese baseball is to not only keep your eye on the ball, but also to keep your eye on the bases and do a fair amount of nimble-footed kicking yourself from time to time. This is rather alien, I think, to our scientific tradition with fixed boundary conditions, clearly defined variables, subjective assessments, and so forth. The point that Ralph was clearly making was that there is no such thing as a stress problem which can be solved for all time and forgotten about, like two plus two is four or other mathematical facts. There are only stress *issues* never fully delineated, never completely resolved, always changing, always in need of alert accommodation. Another cognitive way to cope.

What is stress? Definitions vary widely. For instance, Hans Selye speaks of stress as a non-specific bodily reaction to something out there which may be either stimulating and pleasant or noxious and stressful. Others use the term in exactly the opposite way and speak of stress as that something "out there" which is making us uncomfortable. For me, stress is a rubric that encompasses a stressor, acting on a very complex human organism, usually producing an unhealthy feeling which I think of as a stress reaction.

We will look at three definitions. Stress is a *process* or a system which includes the stressor, a stressful event, a stress reaction, and all the intervening thoughts and feelings and behavior — an overall encompassing rubric. There are two other terms that also require definition. A *stressor* is a stressful event or a stressful condition that produces in the individual a psychological or physical reaction that usually is unpleasant and sometimes causes symptoms of emotional or physical disability. Finally, a *stress reaction* concerns the consequences of the stimulus provided by the stressor. It is, in other words, the response to a stressor, and, as I see it, the stress reaction is usually, but not always, an unhealthy one.

Most often, such reactions can be defined in rather traditional psychological terms ranging from mild situational anxiety or depression to fairly serious emotional disability.

Let's take an example, if we may, that involves all three of these terms. This personal example goes back to the early 1950s when Dr. Kieffer and I were working together in Lexington, Kentucky. I was returning to my home in Lexington by plane. The plane came in for a landing and was about 50 feet off the runway. I could see my family waiting down below — when all of a sudden there was a surge of power and the plane took off again. There was a very terse, single announcement from the cockpit. "The landing gear won't go down." Nothing else. The two stewardesses disappeared into the flight deck. For the next hour and a half there was no word from the flight deck. We flew on to Louisville and circled the tower innumerable times. We could see the fire apparatus lined up below. We could see them spraying foam on the runway. No word from the cockpit.

Talk about stressors. Talk about stress reactions. The term "white knuckle flying" grew out of such experiences. The level of fear and apprehension in the cabin was heightened as we made a final approach with one engine sputtering. The landing was uneventful.

In questioning the captain afterward, I was told that an indicator light had malfunctioned and that it was necessary to obtain visual verification that the nose wheel was indeed locked in place. I asked him why in the world he had not informed his passengers, why the stewardesses had remained up front with him? He was indignant. He seemed nonplused, perplexed that this behavior could be upsetting to anyone. It hadn't occurred to him that the passengers had any need or right to know what was going on, what his plans were, what our degree of jeopardy might be. The lesson from this example is that in times of stress, authority figures (parents, managers) must *be* there. The sheer presence of authority figures who are available to answer questions and to *lead*, is essential. Assurance and reassurance can be drawn from the simple presence of those in command. Dependency needs, in times of stress, are heightened. A demonstration that one's superior cares and recognizes the impact of stress on the employee under his or her supervision will reap incalculable rewards.

How can we organize our thinking about the complex interaction that exists between the individual's ever-changing vulnerability to stressors, and the varying pressures on the job? In what context or environment are specific stressors most apt to produce symptoms? As I see it, there are two factors which determine whether a specific stressor is going to produce symptoms in an individual. The first is the *context* or the external environment in which the interaction takes place. Second, and more important, is the particular *vulnerability* of the individual at the time.

The social, physical, psychological context may be as broad as the economy or as small as the family unit. It may be a single plant in an organization. The main point is that it is external. It is reality based.

In a work setting, the context is also set by management policy and practice, by style of leadership, and the presence or absence of union support. During times of economic uncertainty, with rampant inflation, for example, stressors may be much more significant to the individual than they would be when that individual's economic security is not threatened. The activity of a family unit can be supportive or destructive. I'll come back to that.

Individual vulnerability to specific stressors, of course, varies widely in determining the reactions in a work environment. The enduring personality characteristics of an individual are elements in setting the dimensions of vulnerability. So we must certainly recognize factors such as genetic and developmental influences, as well as the dynamic coping mechanisms each of us uses to adapt and which help to stamp each of us as unique.

At times, vulnerability is heightened. It looms large and one can be much more susceptible to a stressor. At times, it can be relatively insignificant. We can be essentially invulnerable. So the main point is, it varies widely. The impact of events upon the individual varies according to how these events are perceived and the suddeness or unpredictability with which they occur.

One way to illustrate the relationship between context, vulnerability, stressors, and symptoms is by the use of a schematic diagram of overlapping circles. When you look at the diagram of the circles of context, vulnerability, and stressors, (Figure I) they ought to be thought of as constantly moving away from or toward each other, in constant and fluid motion, each varying symbolically in size and with time. If the symbolic circle of vulnerability, for instance, has shifted away from the others to the right so there is no overlap, there would in this schema be no symptoms. The same obtains for environmental factors if the

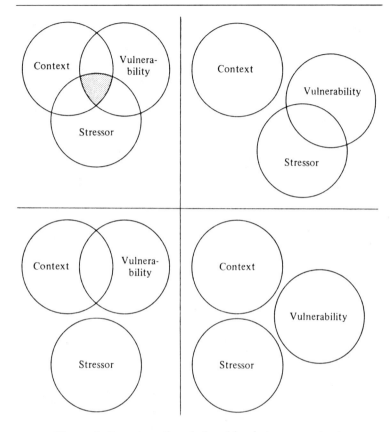

Figure I: Symptomatic relationships between context, vulnerability, and stressors.

context circle moves to the left. In this scheme, contextual or environmental factors obviously contribute to the development of the symptoms. One can withstand otherwise destructive stressors if the context is supportive and the vulnerability is low.

One interesting factor relating to vulnerability comes to us from Johnny Carson who gives us an example by saying that having a sex change operation is traumatic enough, but discovering that one has had such an operation when one goes in for a tonsillectomy is an event of life crisis proportions.

Let me focus on one factor that is extremely important in vulnerability and will serve as an example. This has to do with the particular susceptibility we have, in various stages in life, to various stressors out there. Indeed, each stage of life has its own unique and peculiar vulnerabilities. The various phases of childhood and adolescence each present particular problems of coping and adaptation which the individual must meet and master. So too, the young adult is still growing, maturing, learning, and adapting to the special needs of that age. Each of these periods has its own special crises, its own particular vulnerabilities. So, too, do the later stages of life.

Dan Levinson, at Yale, has suggested a schema which I think is very good (Figure II). He presents it in his book, *The Seasons of a Man's Life* — "man's life," because the study was only of men. He talks about ages 22 to 28 as the early adult transition, and 28 to 33 as entering the adult world. He then discusses the age 30 transition, finally in the late 30s settling down, and finally in the mid-40s, what he calls the mid-life transition. For some, the mid-life transition is a particularly vulnerable time. He carries it further to the late 40s—entering middle adulthood. Then he moves on to the age 50 transition, followed by the combination of middle adulthood, and finally late life transition.

If you think of each of these stages, I am sure you can match up specific susceptibilities or vulnerabilities which are particularly important to the individual at each step. Let me see if I can drive home this point by asking you to remember three numbers: 45, 20, and 40. Herein lie some assumptions about age and certain perceptions that people have. Some can define their very lives by these figures. Forty-five years old, twenty more years to go, $40,000 a year. I hate my job and I'm scared to move! Secure on the outside, making reasonably good money by the national average. Yet the sense of fear is so great that many find themselves literally straight-jacketed. The fears of being over 40 and wondering where you are going to go occupationally can be extraordinarily threatening. Point: not much of a problem at age 30, but of quite a different nature at age 50. Sometimes, it seems to me that management people don't understand this terribly important point. A 55-year-old isn't motivationally, emotionally, or any other way like a 30-year-old.

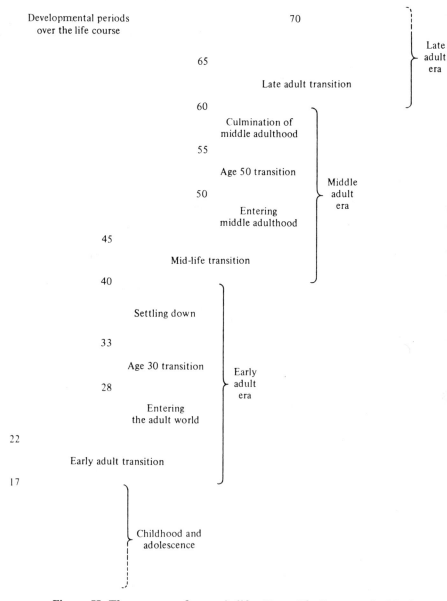

Developmental periods
over the life course

70

65

Late adult transition

60

Culmination of
middle adulthood

55

Age 50 transition

50

Entering
middle adulthood

45

Mid-life transition

40

Settling down

33

Age 30 transition

28

Entering
the adult world

22

Early adult transition

17

Childhood and
adolescence

Late
adult
era

Middle
adult
era

Early
adult
era

Figure II: The seasons of a man's life. (From *The Seasons of a Man's Life*, by Daniel J. Levinson. Copyright © 1978 by Daniel J. Levinson. Reprinted by permission of Alfred A. Knopf, Inc.)

People in work organizations at times tend to think of all employees in a very stereotypical way. Many times they don't *ask* employees about related matters of assignment and work function. It is a little bit like a study done by the Navy during the second World War. The Navy, trying to understand what kinds of people would adapt best to working in the Arctic and in Alaska, performed a whole battery of tests on some 2,000 subjects. It took several days, questionnaires, psychological tests, interviews, and so on. After the individuals were assigned to duty in Alaska, a careful study was done of who did well and who did not, and this information was correlated with the data from the study. It seems that only *one* piece of information from that mass of testing was of any real predictive value. That was a very simple question: "Do you like cold weather?"

Too often we fail to ask people about their preferences, their ideas, and so on. Well, I used the example then of age and stages of life, when talking about vulnerability. If we look at that context circle and at the varying work environments, we might focus on the context in which the work takes place. I said earlier that over the years the changing meaning and nature of work have caused more restructuring of American lives than any force in history, and it is this changing context and meaning of work that also helps determine whether a stressor will produce a stress reaction or be shrugged off, without significant impact.

So, as I see it, the work setting has to be placed in a perspective of external changes that have a bearing on our behavior and our attitudes. For these changes become a part of our work context, and they, in turn, influence how we react to a stressor.

Let me tick off just a few: contemporary economic problems, the dramatic devaluation of the dollar, sky-rocketing inflation, constant change. Two, we seem to be living in an era of rising entitlements. Our expectations have been conditioned by a boom economy in the last few decades. We have cultivated the desire for more and more and a better life. These expectations now seem to have become entitlements in the minds of most workers. We have learned to believe that we deserve direct allocation of resources through the political system as a supplement to the economic system. Third, authority is being increasingly challenged. This clearly has impact on those in management, and, in turn, it affects their family relationships. Fourth, government regulatory agencies seem at times to extend their control without end, exerting incredible pressure on work organizations and those in their management.

Attitudes towards work itself. Take the question, does hard work pay off? In 1967, the majority of American students answered this question, "yes, hard work does pay off." By 1975, fully three-quarters answered the same question, "no." Today, I suspect that the move is back toward a "yes" response, but I have not seen any studies since 1975.

Another part of the changing scene is the increasing legitimacy of being one's self. More than ever it is all right to adhere to one's own values, to reject demands for behavior that runs contrary to them. And increasingly, American business has to recognize and accept that many valuable employees simply will not conform to traditional ways of being managed. More than ever, people are doing their own thing. As I see it, the innovative executive is finding ways to profit from these new values, rather than to contest them.

Finally, part of this changing context that particularly concerns us, is the changing marital states. Marriage has changed dramatically. Traditional marriages, one man and one woman forever, seem to be giving way to more transient relationships of different sorts. One extraordinarily important factor is that marital and sexual ethics and values have changed. One aspect that particularly concerns us when we are talking about work stress is the career family where both partners work and have responsibilities; this has enormous implications for work, for family, for the problems of relocation of the individuals involved.

So much for the broader context of the world in which we live. We've talked a lot about vulnerability and about context. What about specific stressors? I am sure each of you can identify a great many stressors in your work environment and that of family and friends. Therefore, let me simply identify one common denominator, and that is change. Change in the work situation is a common denominator of most stressful events. Changes which are stressful at work and most other places tend to involve loss. Loss may be minor, like giving up comfortable techniques when a work process changes. They may involve irreversible destruction of social bonds, such as when an esteemed supervisor leaves and one whose qualities are unknown comes on the scene. It may be moving from a supportive work group to a competitive hostile one. Or, the loss may be one of self-esteem: when a worker finds himself or herself unable to perform a new and complicated routine. Change, then, seems to be a common denominator for most stressors.

As I said in the beginning, I am not going to propose specific approaches or a solution to problems of work stress. That is the job for some of the rest of the symposium participants. I think that one can keep in mind the concept of vulnerability and think about things which reduce or help to reduce individual vulnerability. I think one can consider context and what one can do to make a situation more supportive of the individual, and I think one can identify and do something about specific stressors.

Now back to another common factor that is very helpful to keep in mind when considering a stress management program. It is the question of asking employees what their views might be. A bit reminiscent of the tombstone in an English country churchyard. It simply said, "I told you I was sick." I'll leave you with an illustration of one of the problems we have in stress management, "He's mad as hell, he has this need to fail, and he keeps on getting promoted."

REFERENCES

Coelho, G. V., Hamburg, D. A. & Adams, J. E. (Eds.) *Coping and adaptation.* New York: Basic Books, 1974.

Grinker, R. R. and Spiegel, J. P. *Men under stress.* Philadelphia: Blakiston, 1945.

Holmes, T. H. and Rahe, R. H. Social readjustment rating scale. *Journal of Psychosomatic Research,* 1967, *11*, 213.

House, J. S. *Work stress and social support.* Alan McLean (Ed.), Addison-Wesley Series on Occupational Stress. Reading, Mass.: Addison-Wesley, 1981.

Levi, L. *Preventing work stress.* Alan McLean (Ed.), Addison-Wesley Series on Occupational Stress. Reading, Mass.: Addison-Wesley, 1981.

Levinson, D. J., Darrow, C. D., Klein, E. B., Levinson, M. H. & McKee, B. *The seasons of man's life.* New York: Knopf, 1978.

McLean, A. A. *Work stress.* Alan McLean (Ed.), Addison-Wesley Series on Occupational Stress. Reading, Mass.: Addison-Wesley, 1979.

Moss, L. *Management stress.* Alan McLean (Ed.), Addison-Wesley Series on Occupational Stress. Reading, Mass.: Addison-Wesley, 1981.

Selye, H. *Stress without distress.* New York: J. B. Lippincott, 1974.

Siu, R. G. H. The Tao of organization management. Chap. 14 in Alan McLean (Ed.), *Reducing occupational stress.* National Institute for Occupational Safety and Health, April 1978. (DHEW) (NIOSH) Publication No. 78-140.

Warshaw, L. J. *Managing stress.* Alan McLean (Ed.), Addison-Wesley Series on Occupational Stress. Reading, Mass.: Addison-Wesley, 1979.

Wolf, S. and Wolff, H. G. *Gastric function: An experimental study of a man and his stomach.* New York: Oxford University Press, 1943.

DISCUSSION

Dr. McLean and Dr. Warshaw conducted a joint panel discussion, "A Psychiatric/Management View," which appears at the conclusion of Dr. Warshaw's speech in the next chapter.

Chapter 2

MANAGING STRESS

Leon J. Warshaw, M.D.*

*Dr. Warshaw, a Board-certified internist who is also certified in Occupational Medicine, has served as Medical Director of Paramount Pictures, United Artists, American Broadcasting Company, and as a consultant on occupational health to a broad range of industrial organizations and governmental agencies. From 1967 through 1980, he was Vice President and Corporate Medical Director of the Equitable Life Assurance Company. Currently, he is Executive Director of the New York Business Group on Health and a consultant on health care to organizations including The World Bank and the British United Provident Association. He has held faculty positions at a number of universities and has lectured widely to both medical and lay audiences. Presently, he is Clinical Professor of Environmental Medicine at New York University. He has been elected a fellow of many professional organizations and serves on the medical advisory boards of such organizations as The American Arbitration Association, The Conference Board, The President's Council on Employment of the Handicapped, The President's Council on Physical Fitness and Sports, and the YMCA's Healthy Back Program. Dr. Warshaw is also a member of the New York Governor's Health Advisory Council. Dr. Warshaw has published over 200 articles in professional and scientific journals, and is the author of three books. The latest, *Managing Stress,* was published by Addison-Wesley.

I am going to address you, not so much as health professionals, but as managers. For, in effect, as providers of health services, you are managers. The operation of a health care facility, operating a program, or running a practice requires management skills. One of the great needs we have in today's crisis in our health care industry is to promote and enhance skills in management. Since, as we have all heard, health care is a labor intensive industry, that means managing people and the problems their interactions present. For example, there are more "blue-collar" workers, if you will, in the health industry, than there are in the unions that Mel Glasser so well represents. (See Chapter 3.)

I will be talking about the work organization—not just business or industry, but any work organization: an organization made up of people working to achieve its mission. It matters little whether it is for profit, not-for-profit, private, or public. One of the best pressure cookers we have with respect to stress and its problems is government itself. As Mel so wisely said, "the major concern of the workers in today's auto industries and in the automated industries is their job security." Anybody who advertises a job having anything even remotely to do with the health field is inundated immediately by scores of applications from people concerned about the Reagan promises of budget cuts in government supported health activities.

What are the impacts of stress on the work organization? In the context of this conference, the most important, of course, is impaired productivity. This is manifested by reduced output, production delays, and most important of all, poor quality of work. I emphasize this because of its great significance. When we think of productivity we almost always think of a worker who turns out a gadget; he is involved in producing something tangible. In the professions and particularly in management, where work involves evaluation and decision making, it is the influence of stress on the quality of those decisions which impacts so strongly on both the organization and the people in it.

A byproduct of impaired productivity is waste, manifested by lost time, equipment breakdowns, and wasted materials. You are, of course, familiar with the three A's that have been the subject of so many earlier South Oaks conferences—absenteeism, due to both sickness and dissatisfaction with work; accidents, which, in effect, so often result from stress; and alcoholism.

Finally, stress leads to poor morale represented by labor unrest, by excessive numbers of grievances, by sabotage, and most important of all, by increased turnover.

In considering how these effects come about and what we may do about them, it is important to refer back to Dr. McLean's presentation and come to a common understanding of what we mean when we use the term "stress." I emphasize the need for a common understanding, because there is perhaps nothing that has been so widely discussed in the medical and lay literature and by news media, that tends to get as misrepresented, befuddled, and stereotyped as the concept of stress. Unless you have an understanding of that basic concept, I defy you to manage it well.

To hark back to Dr. McLean's presentation, the stressor is a stimulus, an event, or a condition that impinges on the individual, while stress is the process through which that stressor affects the individual and causes a reaction. There are many simultaneous stressors and the composite of their effects are what we call stress.

One thing we must remember is that stress is not always harmful. It is not always unhealthy nor is it always unpleasant. In fact, the current spate of horror movies, the popularity of roller coasters, sky diving and so on, really are an indication, if you will, of people's need for some form of stress. Maybe they find it enjoyable because it feels so good when it stops.

How is stress mediated? There are immediate reactions— the neurosympathetic mechanisms, the increased heart rate, the "fight or flight" response of Cannon—these produce an immediate effect which can affect performance. Accuracy, speed, and endurance may be temporarily enhanced, but are usually impaired by the immediate reactions.

We have delayed reactions which involve the hormonal systems—the adrenal corticoids and other hormones—and also emotional reactions which persist. Finally, there are long-term effects, the effects on immune mechanisms, the effect on body processes, which, when deranged, can lead to a variety of diseases that we call "diseases of civilization." These effects, it has been suggested, although not yet proven, may be related to the development of cancer and to the ability to recover from cancer.

To return to Dr. McLean's presentation, we have a host of internal factors which determine our vulnerability. Then, there are a host of external factors which represent the context in which stress functions. The one thing to remember about these is that they do not have boundary lines at the entrance to the workplace. Stress is a continuum 24 hours a day, seven days a week, throughout our lives. In fact, without stress, we do not exist. This emphasizes the truism that we all have an individual capacity—an individual tolerance—for stress, which varies considerably from person to person. Thus, different people react differently to the same level of stress and to the same stressor.

I was reminded by Dr. Sidney Merlis, one of the Planning Committee members for this conference, of some clinical pharmacology studies that we did many years ago in the early days of tranquilizers. We conducted a series of experiments to measure the effects of drugs on the work performance of normal people. We used very small doses of simple tranquilizers as well as small doses of an amphetamine which was a popular stimulant at the time, and measured work performance in terms of output and accuracy in a cohort of entirely normal individuals. On the basis of their past behavior and on the basis of the number of psychophysiologic reactions they had had, we could divide them, albeit somewhat poorly, into two groups of individuals who responded quite differently to the same doses of the same drug. One group showed increased work output, improved accuracy, and experienced a greater sense of well-being. The others, on the same dose of the drug, suffered a decrement of performance and developed symptoms that one could attribute to the drug.

There is really nothing strange about this; you are all familiar with it. It is seen regularly in the bar that Mel Glasser described, the one to which so many workers retire at the end of the day. The individuals treat each other to drinks and are drinking equally—and it doesn't matter what kind of alcoholic beverage they prefer—one soon falls asleep, another gets truculent, and

JOB RELATED STRESSORS

Loss of Job
Loss of job security
Retirement

Change of Job
Relocation
Promotion
Shift work

Defective Job Structure
Inadequate information
Too much competition
Too little cooperation
No input into decisions
Role in organization:
  Role ambiguity
  Role conflict

Inappropriate Job Content
Overload
Underload

Time Constraints
Deadlines
Work hours and conditions

Inadequate Forward Mechanisms
Personal recognition
Promotion
Financial return
Special privileges

Figure I

a third gets sick. Then there is the fellow who goes on talking as though nothing has happened. He is usually the one who is invited to speak on mental health subjects.

Let's examine some of the stressors that are intrinsic to the work setting (Figure I). You have heard some of these before. The most potent—this has been established by repeated studies—is the loss of job *security*. This is more potent than actual loss of the job. One thing that we often forget is that retirement, and impending retirement, actually are a loss of job, a very potent stressor.

Job change is also a potent stressor. This may involve a simple relocation to another part of the plant or a new work site, or a transfer to another part of the city, indeed to another part of the country.

A phenomenon unique to our current era is the stress produced when one worker in a two-career family is being relocated. Is the job change accepted? Is it rejected? Who goes where? I have seen instances when this decision led to divorce; there have been cases of suicide. And very often when the problem may be resolved between the spouses, people neglect to factor in the effect on children who must move with them.

Shift work, especially when shifts are rotated, is a repetitive change of job. And to emphasize that happy occasions may also be stressors, let me remind you that promotion is a change of job. Inappropriate job content is another stressor. Here we speak both of overload and underload. The overload may be quantitative in the sense of just too much work to do, or it may be qualitative in that the work is much too difficult to do. It may involve time constraints: work that is too difficult to do within the deadlines, or work hours that are too prolonged. Also let's not forget that inactivity and boredom are often stressful.

The work environment is another stressor. This involves not only the noise, temperature extremes, and the other toxic hazards in the workplace, but also the social environment. The worker in a noisy shop is not only suffering the effects of noise on his hearing organ, he is also suffering the isolation caused by his inability to communicate with the people working near him.

To continue with job-related stressors, there is the defective structure of the job, the most important of which, perhaps, is inadequate information. What is it I am supposed to do? How am I supposed to do it? And what happens if I don't do it correctly? Too much competition. This is particularly true in management training structures where people are spotted as "quality" personnel, and have to compete with each other as they fight their way up the hierarchy. Too little cooperation. This can be a factor of the way the job is constructed, or it can be a factor of the social climate on the job.

Mel mentioned no input into decisions, and I mention it again to emphasize it. It is most critical, I think. All have ego strengths and ego needs, which dictate that we have some sense of control over what we do and some appreciation that what we do has value. If we are dealt with as automatons or robots and simply assigned to do a task with no opportunity to speak, or at least voice our opinions, even if they do not always carry the day, this can indeed be a potent stressor.

Fogginess about one's role in the organization can be stressful. Role "ambiguity" is a familiar term reflecting uncertain expectations, or a lack of clarity about objectives. We don't know what the scope of our responsibilities is. Role "conflict" is another term that connotes conflicting demands, being forced to do things that we don't like to do. The middle manager, traditionally, is in a position of role conflict in which he has to carry out orders pushed down from above that conflict with his or her sense of how the job should be done, and also conflict with the workers' concept of how they want to do it.

The last and one of the less potent job-related stressors in terms of intensity and importance, even though many people put it at the top of their lists, is the question of rewards, the financial return. There was a time, and it is true again today, thanks to the impacts of inflation, when families needed to have two and three workers to make ends meet and to maintain their living style. But financial return, as an end in itself, very often takes a back seat to such job-related considerations as access to promotion and, more important, personal recognition. Special privileges on the job are a form of recognition but can be stressful when there is inequity in offering them.

While such job-related stressors can be troublesome, it must be emphasized that the major stressors and the major effects of stress come from within ourselves, within our personal and family lives, with the community, and the civilization in which we live. The workplace contributes to them, but not always that significantly. The important thing to remember is that the level of stress in any individual at any given moment is a composite of the effects of all stressors. One cannot separate, one cannot tease out in an individual or a group of individuals that portion of current stress which may be personal, i.e., vulnerability, and which may arise in the context of the community and activities outside the plant, from that arising within the plant. People don't change when they punch the time clock or report to work. They bring to the job all the stressors and all of the stress that they have had in their outside life. Conversely, they take home with them and act out in their family life and in community life and in public life the stress that they accumulate in the workplace.

So, as good managers, we have a number of choices. We

can say, as many managers do, that stress is a personal problem which really doesn't relate to the workplace, and that it is personal and private and we, as managers representing the organization, would be invading privacy to deal with it. Therefore, it is on that worker's head, (or, if psychiatrically oriented, *in* his head). To repeat a phrase, this is known as "indicting the victim"; it serves little use.

On the other hand, there is another approach which is a kind of super-paternalism: to ignore stress and ignore all of these problems until somebody screams in anguish and pain, and then to rush in quickly to ease that individual's discomfort. This involves providing a variety of support mechanisms, all kinds of assistance: throw money at them, throw services at them, weep with and over them. This is known as the "squeaky wheel" approach. It does nothing to get at the basic causes and overlooks what may be far more significant impacts on the totality of the work organization.

The correct approach involves a middle ground in which the individual retains some responsibility for self-help and a variety of support mechanisms are involved, while the sources of stress are identified and controlled before real damage is done. A variety of programs are offered for managing stress in the work setting (Figure II).

The most familiar of those, dealing with individuals already suffering from stress, are known as "the medical models." These seek to identify individuals who are hurting and to induce them to come forward voluntarily or to be referred to professionals who can evaluate their symptoms, diagnose the cause, and offer appropriate treatment. They go under a variety of names and labels: employee health services, counseling services, troubled employee programs, employees' assistance programs, and so on. They range from a telephone hotline, to providing advice in emergency situations, to comprehensive centers that offer an array of services administered by multi-disciplinary professional teams. Some deal with all sorts of problems. Others are focused specifically on such special stress syndromes as high blood pressure, alcoholism, drug abuse, backache, and family problems.

STRESS MANAGEMENT PROGRAMS

Medical Models

Employee health programs
Employee assistance programs
Counseling services
Hypertension, backache, etc.

Reduce Individual Vulnerability

Counseling:
  Individual
  Group
Meditation, relaxation
Exercise programs
Biofeedback
Recreational activities

Reduce Organizational Stress

Supervisor training
Management development
Variable work schedules
Job restructuring:
  Enlargement
  Rotation
  Enrichment
Attitude surveys
Rap sessions

Treat the Organization

Management style
Improve internal communications
Improve planning
Organizational development

Figure II

Next, there is an ever-enlarging group of programs that aim at reducing the vulnerability of the individual. These range from prolonged counseling and formal psychotherapy for those with more fragile personalities, to courses and workshops that purport to teach people to cope more effectively with stress. These have common denominators: training in self-awareness and problem analysis so that the individual is better able to detect signs of increasing stress and to identify the stressors that may be producing it; assertiveness, to become more dynamic in controlling stressors; and techniques that will reduce the stress to more tolerable levels. They include a broad variety of activities: meditation, relaxation programs, exercise programs, biofeedback, and recreational activities.

Then there is the host of programs that are being offered to reduce stress within the work organization. These include attitude surveys, rap sessions and a variety of job-oriented group activities. These are helpful when they work well. But, one word of caution. An attitude survey that offers no feedback on the results of that survey and, even more important, which is not followed by demonstrable, visible, perceptible actions to address some of the problems that are uncovered, is counter-productive. Now that the workplace is becoming a very attractive place for mental health professionals to learn their trade, we see master's degree candidates and Ph.D. candidates come into a workplace and, as an academic exercise, conduct a survey by questionnaire or a series of interviews and then disappear from the scene with nothing happening. The result is usually a profoundly negative reaction and a heightening of stress.

Rap sessions in which a manager sits down with a group of workers and allows them to ventilate their attitudes and perceptions of what is going on can be very useful. But it requires a well trained, sophisticated, and put-together manager to be able to sit in that session and accept the opprobrium that the workers will sometimes throw at him or her. To be able to do so without recrimination and without personally reacting and, especially, to have a follow-on of some kind of action, is critical.

Supervisor training and management development programs are most important. We must get away from the traditional practice of taking the best and most productive worker and making him or her a supervisor, by saying, "OK, you're it and now you do it." This can lead to more difficulty both in terms of a breakdown within that individual, who is suddenly confronted by a total change of responsibility, as well as a breakdown within the work group in adjusting to the new status of one of their peers, however popular he or she may have been before. This person needs training in dealing with "people" problems. Management/supervisor training is faulty if it does not include sensitization to people's communications, both verbal and non-verbal, a sensitization to attitudes that relate to the workplace, to fellow workers, to the supervisor, and to the organization as a whole. Then, having been sensitized, the supervisor must learn what he or she can do to resolve problems that surface.

Variable work schedules are extremely useful and are becoming more and more popular. If they do nothing more than relieve perhaps the most potent stressor in the world of work for many of us who live in crowded urban centers—and that is getting to and from the job—then they are doing a great service. If you come into Manhattan between the hours of 8:00 and 9:00 in the morning and leave between 4:30 and 6:00 in the evening, try, I don't say *ride* the subway, try *to get on* the subway. I know that many of the people who work with me have opted—and they are not over-achievers and they are not workaholics—to be in the office by 8:00 and they never leave before 6:00. The wear and tear is much less than if they commuted at peak rush hours. This again echoes Mel's comments about the blue-collar worker, because most of the people on the subway are blue-collar and white collar-workers, while managers either keep their long hours or ride on the surface (with traffic, this may not be much better!).

Job restructuring seems to have a host of popular names— job enlargement, job rotation, job enrichment, worker democracy; all of these are different names for modifying the content of the job, modifying its structure, and modifying the relationship of one worker to another. In many instances, this has been proposed and implemented as a device to improve productivity, and indeed it does. But I doubt that it does so by any direct effect on productivity, but rather one that is mediated through the workers' better sense of well-being and relief from needless stress.

The last category deals with the organization as a living system. A corporation is legally a person, and when we are forced to deal with it as a person, we often recognize that it has its own personality, its own vulnerability, and it operates in the context of government regulations, the economic crisis world trade problems, the falling value of the dollar, what is happening in the stock market, and so on. But in the last analysis, it is made up of people. Therefore, we must deal with it as a living system that needs guidance in deploying and coordinating its resources to cope more effectively with changes in both its internal and external environments. This involves programs that deal with faulty communications—perhaps the most frequent source of organizational conflict—with inappropriate management style, with effective planning that establishes realistic attainable objectives and expectations, and, most importantly, with mechanisms to neutralize the effects of personal difficulties of strategically-situated managers whose actions and decisions, or inability to make them, create problems for everyone in the organization. The last is particularly needed when there has been a change in management, when the chief executive officer is succeeded, or when a company is absorbed into a conglomerate and now has to change its personality and adapt to an entirely new world.

The concept labeled "Organizational Development" is intended to be a program, carried on over years, that has a feedback loop which evaluates the performance of the organization as an entity and the key people within it. It then modifies their behavior and their relationships through better planning, and then re-evaluates the result.

I have presented you with a long list of programs for managing stress within the organization. As Dr. McLean indicated, those of you in professional or managerial positions are inundated with letters, flyers, ads, and calls from people who are purveying one or another kind of a program as though *it* is *the* answer. How do you select the program or programs most suitable for the organization? Well, one way is to think of it in terms of the menu for a family dinner in a Chinese restaurant. You pick two from Column A and one from Column B, and so on down the line. This produces a menu which is not altogether unpalatable.

Another way is to let the price decide. If you have a budget, you know how much you can spend. Then you pick the one that you can afford to buy and don't worry about the others.

Perhaps the usual way in which organizational managers solve this dilemma is to ride the crest of the wave and pick the best seller—the program that has been featured in Time, Newsweek, The Harvard Business Review. The Wall Street Journal is a superb place to learn about the most current panacea.

Oddly enough, it really doesn't matter, because all of these will work, at least to some extent, and for a time. Virtually every kind of program will provide some benefit to at least some of the people exposed to it. It may be the placebo effect. It may be just the good will induced by the evident desire of the organization to be helpful. It may be the ethyl-chloride, the freezing spray that the trainer puts on the bruised athlete that dulls the pain and enables him to go on and perform. Because we are dealing with an ever-changing world in which people are changing too, it is entirely possible that the observed benefits may have resulted from unrelated extraneous factors rather than any stress management program.

The correct approach is more complicated than blindly picking a program out of the bucket. It requires a study of the organization and its personnel in the context of the industry and the context of the community of which they are a part. It requires assessing the current and potential impact of stress and identifying the predominant stressors. It requires a commitment of the organization to really do something about them. It requires the allocation of resources, in terms of man-hours or dollars to buy man-hours of expert help—this presumes the availability of people who are qualified to launch and conduct a program, often a critical consideration. With that kind of approach—it is nothing more than the classic "evaluation, decide, try, and evaluate" rubric—one can be most certain of a good long-term approach.

There are some axioms for the manager who wants to control stress within the organization. First and most important is to *know* the people. It is critical in larger organizations to pay attention to who the people arc and where they come from. My current experience as a consultant for The World Bank is a classic example. The World Bank recruits its staff from more than 100 countries that are members of the bank. They come from all over the world, more recently from third world countries, and they bring their families with them. An extraordinarily potent stressor is their need to accommodate and adjust to the urban

American scene in Washington, D.C.. A program that simply provides them with the kind of diet that will satisfy their cultural and ethnic palates, in itself is a major stress-reliever.

In that context you may be interested in an anecdote. Some of you may know Gouverneur Hospital, one of our city's oldest and most illustrious institutions which is now a repository for elderly, chronic-care individuals, many of whom are Chinese. Perhaps it is one of the signs of our times; it didn't happen when I was on the staff at Bellevue years ago. In my day the Chinese took care of their own and one rarely saw them in chronic-care institutions of any sort. Now there is a sizeable population of elderly and disabled Chinese who are patients at Gouverneur. Largely reflecting language barriers and cultural differences, a profound discontent permeated the Chinese patient population. This spilled out into the staff, who became resentful. Actual battles were fought because the Chinese patients felt that there was indifference to their needs on the part of the staff and the administration. Research was done to identify the most potent stressors that might be addressed within the current fiscal constraints.

One was found. And its control alloyed a whole host of anxieties and resentments and brought calm to those waters. I challenge you to guess what it was. They got a chef who could cook Chinese rice. There are rice cookers that will produce Chinese-style rice, but they only make very small quantities at a time and here was a sizeable population to be fed on the hospital's schedule. The hospital administrator, being a very aggressive and ingenious individual, found a fellow who had worked in a Cuban restaurant (now, for the first time, I understand why, when one goes around certain areas in Manhattan, one finds "Cuban-Chinese" restaurants) who was accustomed to preparing Chinese rice. With that, the problem eased so that nothing more was needed.

My second precept is to know the workplace, to know the work environment, to know what is going on and particularly what is about to happen.

The third is to observe and listen. One of our local organizations has been on national TV promoting a program on how to listen. This is long overdue. Our skills as health professionals are based on our ability to observe and listen. But we also need a caring attitude, to be approachable, and to recognize that many people are ashamed of or very sheepish or concerned about revealing their stress reactions, lest they be thought of as deficient or defective.

Of critical importance is professional competence as a manager. I am not talking now about competence as a health professional, but as a manager. Professional competence as a manager includes knowing what to do and what not to do about people problems, avoiding flip stereotyped responses, emphasizing the quality of referrals, and not being seduced by fads and quacks.

Equally important is maintaining one's integrity: integrity as an individual, as a manager, and as a representative of the organization. This means that one must never sacrifice an individual to the organization. One must be an advocate for what is right, not necessarily for what people want, and particularly as a manager, one must be even-handed. Inevitably, managers tend to be apologists for management. They are part of the team and part of the decision-making process. But there comes a point at which one must stop being an apologist. As a manager, one can sometimes ease the hurt of management decisions, but when they are unwise or unfair there may be no other way of dealing with them except by some kind of aggressive action, even if it involves risk. And very often managers, today, solve that dilemma to their personal advantage by moving on to another job in another place.

The most important aspect of management involvement is education—to educate the organization and the individuals on all levels with respect to stressors, their effects, and what can be done not only to cope but, more importantly, to prevent.

Finally, what are the manager's responses to stress? (Figure III). We start with good working conditions and reasonable job assignments. Keep competition at reasonable levels. Maintain firm, fair discipline that is understood by all. Provide adequate support. Be sure that directions are clear. Provide appropriate incentives which include personal recognition, economic rewards, and promotion. And most important of all, echoing the plea that

THE MANAGER'S RESPONSES TO STRESS

Competition at reasonable levels
Firm, fair discipline that is understood
Provide adequate support
Directions—clear cut
Appropriate incentives and rewards:
  Personal recognition
  Economics
  Promotion
Human dignity

Figure III

Mel so eloquently expressed, have a sense of and a dedication to the preservation of human dignity. Without that, our organizations are meaningless.

REFERENCES

House, J. S. *Work stress and social support.* Addison-Wesley Series on Occupational Stress. Reading, Mass.: Addison-Wesley, 1981.

Levi, L. *Preventing work stress.* Addison-Wesley Series on Occupational Stress. Reading, Mass.: Addison-Wesley, 1981.

McLean, A. A. *Work stress.* Addison-Wesley Series on Occupational Stress. Reading, Mass.: Addison-Wesley, 1979.

Moss, L. *Management stress.* Addison-Wesley Series on Occupational Stress. Reading, Mass.: Addison-Wesley, 1981.

Shostak, A. *Blue collar stress.* Addison-Wesley Series on Occupational Stress. Reading, Mass.: Addison-Wesley, 1980.

Warshaw, L. J. *Managing stress.* Addison-Wesley Series on Occupational Stress. Reading, Mass.: Addison-Wesley, 1979.

DISCUSSION

Dr. McLean and Dr. Warshaw chaired a joint panel discussion of stress from a psychiatric/management viewpoint. Panel discussants were: Leonard S. Brahen, Ph.D., M.D., Medical Di-

rector, Nassau County Department of Drug and Alcohol Addiction; Patrick F. Carone, M.D., M.P.H., Assistant Director,
Professional Education, South Oaks Hospital; John J. Dowling,
M.D., M.P.H., Commissioner, Nassau County Department of
Health; Irving Hammerschlag, M.D., Medical Director, Long Island Lighting Company; and David Harris, M.D., M.P.H., Commissioner, Suffolk County Department of Health Services.

Dr. Warshaw:

This is a dual panel discussion involving a psychiatric/man-
agement view of stress and productivity.

I am going to give you a laboratory in stress and stress tolerance by putting the spotlight on the panelists. I am going to
ask each of them —either as individuals or as managers or as
professionals—to identify for you what they feel are the three
most common or most potent stressors that affect work and productivity. They will then be free to make any and all extended
remarks for no more than two or three minutes each. If you
have ever heard of a stressful assignment, this is it.

The outward equanimity of the panelists who have received
this assignment tells you a very important thing—that the ster-
eotype of a person under stress, who is quivering, shaking, pale-
faced, fidgeting and so on, is not always the person under a great
deal of stress. Rather, sometimes the individual who sits stolidly,
stone-faced, unmoving, is so shocked by the stress that he or she
is driven into that corner.

Dr. Brahen:

I would like to look at stress from the point of view of young
people who have had employment difficulties or cannot sustain
employment or often cannot even be employed. This has to do
with their very low response threshold to stress. Often we see
individuals who can tolerate very little stress or frustration; their
tolerance is low and, for example, if the boss says something to
them they capsize or say the "wrong" thing. It is very important
for industry to look at the individual employee. Employee mis-
takes are made when one cannot tolerate anxieties produced by
employment. We find in our own clinic that many young people
use drugs to handle stress and anxiety. Sometimes the doctor

can reduce the anxieties produced by the stressful situation and the patient can make it through. Oftentimes the patient has insufficient ego strength and gets caught up in an addiction.

Dr. Carone:

I would like to enumerate what I consider to be the three greatest causes of emotional stress on the job.

First, I would identify the confusion of task or job ambiguity that many people are subjected to, as one of the greatest sources of stress and one of the great sources of conflict on the job. The second one which, at first glance, may not appear to be a stress, but which I believe is, is boredom, particularly for people who are involved in jobs that involve repetitive tasks with little variation and little gratification in terms of seeing the finished product. The assembly-line worker is a prime example of this; putting the oil pan on the bottom of an automobile, doing that one task over and over. The third issue involves a distinction between stress and stimulation. It is a curious property of the human being that, while uncomfortable levels of stimulation constitute stress, people nevertheless seek some level of stimulation. The question of the boundary line beyond which stimulation becomes stress is a very important factor.

Dr. Hammerschlag:

My particular interests are environmental medicine and ergonomics. Ergonomics is a method of being productive in a tiresome, boring procedure. If you have to tighten the same nut all day long, something is going to go wrong, something has got to give. In the 6,000 people who work for us, I've observed a "disease" which expresses itself as headaches, disturbances in sleep, generalized aches and pains, shortness of breath, chest pains, confusion, difficulty in staying awake, and every other possible medical symptom we can think of. These symptoms all have a common denominator called *stress.*

Dr. Harris:

If I were to choose one thing that sums up many stressors in the work situation, it is the failure of management to take into account human factors, human feelings. There isn't a technique mentioned by Dr. Warshaw for stress management that isn't also a good technique for everyday good management. Discrimination in the workplace—whether it is based on race, sex or age—is an important source of stress and something which can be remedied by management with good personnel policies.

The last point I would like to make, in terms of the human factor in stressors is diversity. Management has opportunities to relieve stress by taking advantage of human diversity. Some people delight in stress; they just eat it up. An important management tool is not to *fit* people into the organization but sometimes to build your organization around people with various talents. While this is probably more possible at the white-collar level, there is some room for this at the blue-collar level as well. Using the scientific methods that we have available or can develop, we can plan the right jobs for the right people.

Dr. Dowling:

Both Dr. McLean and Dr. Warshaw mentioned that there were three factors involved in their stress concept: vulnerability, contact stressor, and stressor process and reaction. There is a similarity to the ingredients of the concepts they put forth, and those of us who have been trained and have some understanding of epidemiology, were glad to hear the threesome come out again—the agent, the host, and the environment. We realize that there are multiple factors and one of the important ones is the individual.

I happen to believe that one of the most important ingredients, if not *the* most important, is the individual, in this case the worker. What are the qualities, the values, the background, the family structure, the society, the culture, that cause certain individuals to become stressful in situations where others are calm. What are the factors that enable some people to thrive, to grow, to respond so well to change, while other individuals are destroyed by change? What are the particular differences?

In the health care field, personnel have, it is hoped, the education, the training, the knowledge, and the background to be aware of and to provide services to the community. But, as managers, what is our responsibility for the needs of our employees?

As they get into stressful situations, we have the responsibility for the "what" (what kinds of services). Is the individual doing a good job—concentrating on the "what"? The "why" (why am I doing this) is also important. You have to have sensitivity, you have to have awareness of the "why." What is it about a particular employee that enables one to do a better job? What qualities are present? And when the employee stops serving effectively, how far do we go, as employers, as managers, in helping the employee? At what point do we say you can't continue in this particular job any longer. You are going to have to be relieved, transferred, or get help, because you are no longer effectively producing.

Dr. McLean:
    Much of what we have heard has had to do with stressful *events.* I think it would be interesting to divide our thinking among those factors in a work environment which are steady state, those which are stable, and those which I would call stressful *conditions,* as well as those changes which represent stressful *events.* I think we can usefully compartmentalize our thinking, whether it be based on a one-to-one clinical workup of a given individual, or whether it be based on work groups or work organizations, because there are a number of ongoing conditions. Dr. Carone mentioned one when he talked about machine-paced work which is, for some, a constant condition and a very unpleasant aspect of employment. I would toss in just one other. When an individual's value system, for instance, is different from the value system of the work organization, this can create all kinds of problems in and for that individual. Many times a person is locked into that kind of situation; he can't get away if other jobs aren't readily available. This can cause a tremendous amount of anxiety and conflict.
    I was trying to think of what kinds of jobs were the most stressful. A totally extraneous thought popped into my head: it must be the jobs of those individuals in Norway and Sweden who are charged with implementing legislation that mandates non-stressful work.

Dr. Warshaw:

One of the profound stresses or stressors that one will en-counter in the work setting or in other places is loss of control over a situation. Clearly, the way to avoid work stress is to be in control of the job. If I can decide what I am going to do and when I am going to do it, at what speed, and set my own stand-ards for quality, then I am not likely to be too stressed. On the other hand, if suddenly I find myself under the sway of a mentor or a supervisor or a top executive or a govenment inspector who now holds up a completely different set of criteria or standards on which I am to be judged and makes me do things at someone else's timing, then I don't control the work, the work controls me. And this can happen intellectually as well as physically.

I shrink and shudder every time I see in print, the term, "the compliance of the patient." One reason we are seeing so much stress in the helping professions is because the great public is no longer as "compliant" as they might be. They want to have some control over what is going on in their lives, in their work, and with their health. They want to be consulted and advised as to the alternatives. They want to know what the incentives, the rewards or the drawbacks are, and they want to be part of the decision-making process. We are seeing a call for democracy in health care services as well as in the workplace and I happen to think that this is very necessary.

Audience:

I'm with Grumman Aerospace Corporation and I would like to ask if you could describe a model environment that is pro-ductive and positive. It seems that all we have heard about is what is wrong with the environment. What is one that people work well in?

Dr. Harris:

If, by a model environment, you mean a totally stress-free environment, I must admit that I couldn't find one. As a matter of fact, I might go so far as to say that not only would a stress-free environment be unstimulating, it would be boring. A lack of challenge commensurate with skill and ability turns out to be a stressful condition in the broader sense of the word.

The model is an organization in which the working force participates in deciding how work will be organized and how it will be carried forward. You can look at many organizations and, if that yardstick is more or less met, you will have a good example of the ideal.

Dr. Warshaw:

Even though a manager could produce an environment with an ideal level of stress, one must not forget that much of the stress at work comes from social interaction, from the people themselves. Here we have many individual characteristics brought together. Until we all turn into computers or robots, there will still be individuality, and this in itself can make for work stress.

I am reminded of a trip in an elevator in a Manhattan office building where I heard a young lady complaining most vociferously. She said, "Damn it, every time I really get into my job there is a coffee break and I have to quit." I caught her in the corridor and asked her why she didn't just stay on the job. She said, "If I didn't take the coffee break, my co-workers would be on my neck." A lot of stress is actually man-made.

Audience:

One aspect of stress that wasn't mentioned was shift work.

Dr. Warshaw:

Clearly, shift work is stressful in terms of the biological rhythms that are so very important. We see this when we travel east-west in fast flights, and our day-night cycle is changed. Laboratory tests have shown that it takes about 72 hours for most body functions to reach a normal level on the new time frame.

With shift work, people are out of phase. It takes a while to adapt. Once they have made the adaptation, the predominant problem is not so much their basic physiology, but that they are socially out of tune. People have difficulties sleeping in the daytime, not so much because of the light, but because of the noise. Their social and family lives are disrupted.

The most stressful form of shift work is rotating shifts where time frames are constantly changing. Our late friend and colleague, Dr. David Goldstein, did an interesting study at The New York Times. He tracked the accident rate among the pressroom workers and discovered that the peak rate of accidents regularly occurred on the day following a shift change. In other words, after a two-week period, the workers had gotten fairly well indoctrinated to their present rhythm. Then they had a hiatus, a long weekend, and came back on a different shift. It was on their return to work, following a shift change, that accidents occurred. This presumably reflected their inability to make that biological adjustment in so short a time.

Dr. Harris:

If it is not of your own choosing, even a stable shift tends to be more stressful. For example, at hospitals there are certain individuals whose social life and personality and way of handling things makes them ideal for night or evening work. But the greatest stress, at least as measured by poor performance, grievances, and unhappiness that the supervisors detect, occurs when people are on a shift they don't like. They may have been assigned to it merely because of lesser seniority. These people have the most trouble with the stress created by unusual shifts, such as nights or evenings.

Dr. Warshaw:

Of course, there are some who do much better on various shifts; for example, the person who likes to surf-cast or the one who wants to be home when the kids come home from school. Some people like the night shift because it is quieter, everybody else is asleep, and supervision tends to be more relaxed. Again we come back to the individual and the danger of stereotyping.

Audience:

You are all obviously experts in stress. I know you are aware of it on the job, but how about when you go home and have to deal with your family. You are all aware of the tremendous effect of stress on a family.

Dr. McLean:

It may be a sign of masochism to respond. But I would invoke most of the variables that we have touched on in terms of underlying principles of stressor and stress reaction. It depends on how vulnerable we are at that particular time to the stresses at home. It depends on how much sleep we got the night before. It depends on what our current relationship is with our spouse or our children. It depends on what crisis may have come up at home that we hadn't anticipated.

Dr Brahen:

Some of us go home infrequently. We are compulsive workers who may avoid stressful situations at home by overworking. Nevertheless, we are successful workers, often by virtue of our compulsiveness.

Audience:

I am a nursing home admininstrator. Participation as a way of eliminating stress doesn't always work. I know of a situation, for example, where labor was invited by management to participate in policy-making decisions, and the invitation was rejected because the workers said that management was merely seeking to share the blame for their incompetence.

Dr. Warshaw:

As the song goes, "It takes two to tango!" Participation management works only when both labor and management are committed to making it work.

Audience:

One of the frustrations of the worker in a larger company is that he or she cannot reach the person who has the last word. The worker has to deal with people on many levels of management, all of whom say, "I can't help it because I've got a set of rules too." This is very frustrating. In my youth, we were able to talk to the boss who might say, "yes" or "no," but at least we knew where we stood.

Another conflict that a person has today is dealing with the "tapes" in his head pertaining to his religious responsibility, his morality, the rules and regulations by which he should live, and the peer pressures which are tearing him away from those spiritual values. He has to face these in the workplace as well as at home and in his social life.

These two problems cause a tremendous amount of stress.

Dr. Warshaw:

I can extend that comment by asking how many of you have suffered the stress of trying to get a correction made on one of your credit card or charge accounts?

Dr. Harris:

I would like to address the first of your problems. As organizations have gotten larger, this has become an even greater source of stress in the work situation. I sometimes call it the "Franz Kafka Castle Syndrome." One approach that has been taken is a decentralization of authority. In an organization where nobody can give you a definitive answer until you get to the top, the authority to make those decisions needs to be moved closer to the front lines. Generally, the solutions to that problem are organizational.

Dr. Carone:

In a number of places where I have worked, I have seen a variety of organizational structures. Some of them seem to work and you can get your answers, and some of them don't seem to work. One factor is the issue of consonance of goals and consonance of tasks. It has been my impression that when someone is trying to perform a function, *especially* a human service function, the goal identified by the worker may differ from the goal identified by the organization. Much of the apparent inefficiency and impaired communication is an unspoken, but more or less intentional, manipulation.

It has always fascinated me that one of the most difficult jobs in medicine, particularly in psychiatry, is to be the first person on the scene with the sick patient. The psychiatrist who sees patients in the emergency room or in the clinic is not the chief of the department or a senior psychiatrist who is most expert. It is not the senior resident who has had three years of experience, but it is the first-year resident who knows the least who is given the responsibility of making what, in most cases, are very difficult decisions. This is one of the issues where communication is more or less intentionally confounded because of the divergence between the tasks and goals of the worker and the management.

Audience:

It seems that people will be stressed and distressed regardless of what environment we create. Therefore, is it not the responsibility of employers to help identify those people who are distressed and provide the kind of rehabilitation which will make them better and more productive people?

Dr. Harris:

That comment is well taken. I would say, although it is beyond the scope of this particular conference, that there is need for prevention. Dr. Dowling mentioned the agent, host, and environment model. We have been talking mostly about either the agent—the job situation—or the environment, which may be the home, the community, or the economy.

There is something that can be done, not to "immunize" people so that they are able to tolerate more stress, but "teach" them about stress. The way people are brought up, how they achieve successes in their early life, how they handle stress successfully in their early life, their feeling of self-worth—these things determine whether people are better able to stand a particular degree of stress. I think it is the responsibility of management to assist in identifying individuals with problems and to assist them in getting the help they need.

Managements throughout this country are increasingly aware that they are spending enormous amounts of money on benefits for some of the problems through which stress emerges. These include alcoholism, and various mental problems. Intervention would not only reduce those expenditures, but would also heighten productivity.

Audience:

There must be some way parents can learn how to help their children to acquire the skills needed to deal with stress. This could be expanded in the schools and later on in the workplace. Thus, coping with stress would be part of adjusting to life. Reducing stress usually works against adjustment. If every time there is a stressful situation, we remove it, people will not learn to deal with stress. How can we help parents, teachers, or doctors to increase the capacity of the individual to deal with stress?

Dr. Harris:

The key to prevention is *not* to immunize a person against stress, but to strengthen the person so that stress can be handled. Now, I don't believe that stress-management classes should be taught in school. What I do think, though, is that if the attitude of parents in their child-rearing practices, and the attitude of teachers as they approach their students, generates mutual respect, real respect for the students and for children, that would be a *positive* contribution to handling stress. Other things can be done in a more mechanistic nature. You don't give people the kind of stress that leads to certain failure. If that is done repeatedly in the early years of life, it may well ensure difficulty with stress as an adult.

Dr. Brahen:

Yes, people are different. As we standardize jobs in large industries—and we do need to do this for efficiency—we have to be aware that people bring different ego-strengths to the job. A particular challenge could be rewarding for one employee and devastating for another. As we move into the mechanized age, we have standardized jobs that are rather impersonal. Workers, though, are not robots.

Dr. Warshaw:

With respect to the school system, if one believes some critics, children in school don't learn to read. They don't learn to write. What they do learn is the ability to cope with stress in the "blackboard jungle." So, perhaps inadvertently and accidentally, they are indeed in a stress laboratory.

Dr. Hammerschlag:
    A factor we have to deal with is the adequacy of one's training for the specific job that he or she is going to perform. Thorough preparation to perform that job decreases many of the problems that must be dealt with. Many people have jobs that have nothing to do with their basic education.
    One of the problems I've heard time and time again is, "When I get the answers, they change the questions." A serious problem in industry occurs when a person does not know what he or she has to do. In order to be in a non-stressful or limited stress situation, people must know just what job they have to perform. If they know it, they have two options, either they do it well or they don't do it well. I have found in our company that the individual you report to should not be six stages above your position. He should be one of you. If you are on the line crew, then let the lowest foreman be your boss, and he will report to another foreman and so on up the line. I find that this is a situation most people can live with quite adequately.

Audience:
    Would it be feasible to add another component to your job description that would analyze the emotional factors of the job?

Dr. Hammerschlag:
    It sure would. But it is a question of spending the money or having the right personnel to evaluate an individual so that he really fits into his job. In general, this is done; his training and his background are evaluated, but there is certainly a great deal of room for improvement. Eventually it will almost become a science and people will be trained to put the right person in the right job.

Dr. Warshaw:
    Increasing attention is also being paid to tailoring the job to the individual. It works both ways: The square peg in the round-hole syndrome can be cured by shaving down the sides of the square peg or reaming out the hole.

Audience:

I am a nurse administrator at a state psychiatric hospital. More emphasis should be put on flexibility of shifts. If a person could come in, say, an hour later or an hour earlier without conflict in the operation of the institution, it would benefit the employee *and* the organization.

Dr. Warshaw:

At Equitable Life, where I worked for some years, any work unit, by a vote among the workers in that unit, could opt for any kind of work shift or work schedule that met their fancy, as long as it didn't interfere with performance. In other words, if you worked in the mailroom and you had to be there when the post office dumped the sacks of mail and you also had to get the sacks into the post office, then your hours were externally determined. The result was that many people had variable schedules; some had flextime in which they came and went at any hour that suited them; some worked early shifts, some late shifts; some had four-day weeks; others alternated long weekends; and so on. Some units that tried an alternative work schedule discovered that they didn't like it so much and voted to go back to their original hours. It is a form of worker democracy that was encouraged and tolerated by management as long as it didn't interfere with work flow. Increasingly, organizations are finding ways to do that.

Audience:

Is there any difference between the stress that the employee working for industry experiences and that of the worker who is within the bureaucracy?

Dr. Warshaw:

I recently spent two-and-a-half years as a consultant to the Mayor of New York. During this time the New York City government was embattled and in crisis. There are several differences between the stress experienced by industry employees and that of bureaucratic employees. In private industry, the major stress felt by many managers is the "bottom line"—the annual audit, the annual stockholder's statement, where you are at the end of that period. In the world of government, where the managers are not civil servants, but elected or appointed officials, the bottom line is the next election. In both situations, this tends to militate against long-term planning, and it makes for expediency; putting Band-Aids on problems rather than really trying to resolve them. Now, both in government and in the private sector, managers are increasingly recognizing that problems are not usually resolved that quickly and they are getting involved in long-range planning and developing strategies to overcome these problems once and for all.

Audience:

I am one of the chaplains at South Oaks. As a paster, I have counseled both management and those in the labor force, and I find that, in some situations, they have "givens" that they cannot alter for a year or two. What type of resources or approach can the mental health professionals give to an employee who has certain "givens," who has to live in a situation where there is distress? How can he use stress in a creative way and become productive?

Dr. Carone:

To look at that question, I will put it into a different context where there are fewer variables. Take the situation back to the time when a person is one or two years of age and when the task at hand—in other words, the production deadline—is control of one's bladder and bowels. To become toilet trained is a task which is imposed by management, Mother and Dad. This task is highly valued by society, particularly by people who visit. Eventually, it has a creative potential for the employee who is working at the task.

I think the issues are that indeed some sort of a mandate comes down, the task becomes defined, there is a communication of the task from the employer to employee. In most families, it is a situation which comes about without too much difficulty. It is both stimulating and stressful to the child and results in a creative process which constitutes part of the formation of the child's psyche. But even this simple situation is complex. What if the parents are socially conscious and ambitious and they are the type of people who decide they want their child trained at a year and a half? And what if the neurologic apparatus isn't ready to be trained? Then you have an unfair, undue kind of stress. You are asking the child to do something he can't. This results in interpersonal conflict anxiety, defiance, and makes, no pun intended, quite a messy situation. If the parental management attitude is different and the situation takes place later, with the child missing his opportunity to train at the earliest possible time—assuming that that is an advantage—then there is again an unfair situation in which the child's potential is not reached. He is placed in a job beneath his capacity.

So, even a simplified situation like that is rather complex. However, the principles are the same. If you are dealing with an adult who is in a difficult situation that has to be endured for some period of time—be it an untenable marriage or an untenable job position—what are the coping mechanisms? The unpleasant and perhaps unnecessary stress is there and isn't going to go away, and the person has to endure it.

In a similar way to the child learning how to toilet train, this involves a certain kind of growth and creativity; learning how to use inner resources and values, developing a philosophical approach, permitting outlets for ventilation, and permitting displacement of the conflict into other areas where some mastery can be achieved. Such as physical exercise, sports, or throwing darts. These represent psychological coping mechanisms which can be effective. As a minister, you have access to certain tools that I don't, because you can predicate other kinds of equally beneficial resources and meanings to the events.

Audience:
    As a teacher, I am aware of the problems of youngsters. Children come to us to be educated, often with a very negative attitude toward authority. Our permissive society perpetuates this. Our basic family unit often is not intact. We have a lot of fatherless children. We have a lot of children who are raised by grandparents. We have seen our religious values go downhill. So what is left? The schools. How far do we go? Somebody really

has to be the boss. Somebody has to be secure. Somebody always has to be there. So who is there? The teacher.

What does the teacher do? Encourage the child's basic strengths. We *are* learning to cope with stress in the school system. We *are* teaching the children. I do stress exercise in my third-grade classroom. I teach the children to relax. I try to teach them to look at themselves in a very positive way. We want the children to have a good self-image and to mature as adjusted adults who will be able to handle stress and be able to produce.

Audience:

I am a psychotherapist and I do consulting for employee assistance programs and occupational alcoholism programs. I have a two-point question. The first part has to do with my difficulty in holding on to the notion of when stress becomes distress and when distress becomes stress. I was wondering if there is any work being done to quantify those concepts. Since we are saying stress is a part of life and everybody needs some, how much does the average person really need? It may help, in terms of the theme of stress and productivity, to know what levels of stress are indeed optimal for production and what levels of distress, if you will, are most limiting in terms of production.

The second part of my question is addressed to Dr. Brahen. In my limited experience with adolescent drug abusers, I find there is very little stress in their early years of development. There is oftentimes an overprotective parent and a kind of pathological symbiosis that goes on between parent and child. Then, the stress of adolescence becomes overwhelming as opposed to being on a continuum. When the stress of adolescence is added to the stress or distress of the pathological symbiosis, drugs become a way of dealing with this distress.

Dr. Brahen:

You bring up an important point in regard to adolescent alcoholism and drug abuse. Although they mean well, some parents handle children in such a way that the child does not develop adequately. In a psychodynamic sense, the child is crippled. The parents may give a lot to the children in terms of time and material goods. They may involve themselves more than is good for the child. We may then see a so-called good parent, who does too much and emotionally cripples the youngster. To use a comparable example in medicine, take someone with a fractured leg who is put in a cast and never given the opportunity to again use the limb. If he is always moved about in a wheelchair, he will never learn to walk. It may be well-meaning but it certainly doesn't serve the individual and the individual's strength within himself.

In terms of the dynamics of separation and individualization, the child doesn't become separated, and therefore develops many problems. Many times the child lives with his parents or may even live away from them, but in either case, he has not separated from his parents. These children may run off to California, but they haven't separated. Their need to be independent is often demonstrated by taking alcohol. One has to look at the youngster and parent together. Parents oftentimes do not see what they are doing; which is not permitting the child to grow. It may have been satisfactory at year one, two, three, or four, but it is not appropriate when the youngster is a teenager.

As to quantifing the amount of stress that one can take, I think it has to do, again, with genetics. We have some youngsters who just cannot work, no matter how easy the work is. We have some schizoid individuals who experience so much anxiety in just living that they never get around to working, or fail at work quickly.

Dr. Warshaw:

In response to your first question about quantifying stress, I suggest that in university libraries there are probably more than 1,000 Ph.D. theses that describe instruments for measuring stress. There are probably 10,000 master's theses concerned with developing stress-measurement instruments. There is even greater lay literature—I refer you to such illustrious magazines as The Reader's Digest, Women's Day, Cosmopolitan, etc., that feature self-scoring tests. The answer is that we don't have a useful measure for stress. We can measure the intensity of some specific stressors, such as the intensity of noise and isolation. We can measure stress responses: heart rate, catechol excretion and a variety of physiologic functions, such as nerve conduction, etc. We can measure various performances through tests of one kind or another, such as simple arithmetic, spelling, or following a maze. They all measure something finite.

But when we talk about the intact individual, in the complicated world in which he lives and works and rests, we have yet to find a measurement device which will give us a useful quantification.

Dr. Harris:

I agree that pure measurements of the intensity of a stressor, or the ability of a given stressor to cause a certain quantum of stress in an individual is a meaningless kind of measurement, unrelated to both the host, that is, the individual being stressed, and also the environment, that is, the context in which the stress is applied to that individual. At certain times one man's pleasure is another man's pain. Someone asked a little earlier about the difference between stimulation and stress. Well, I suppose you could say that if a man is winked at by a pretty girl, that is stimulation. And if he is winked at by a pretty girl with his wife in the same room, that's stress.

I have a summer home in Maine and once I was at a meeting where former Senator Muskie was speaking and he told a story of a friend of his who came from a large eastern city where he was in the advertising business and at the same time ran his own retail business. He found both of these far too stressful, so he went to rural Maine where the major industry is potato growing. Later Senator Muskie said he met his friend and asked him, "How is the rural life, how is it going?" "Terrible. I quit my job." "I thought you went to Maine to get rid of stress." "I did." "What did you do?" "I worked on a potato farm." "Were you the manager of the potato farm?" "No, I was a sorter; I stood by the potato conveyor belt and as the potatoes came by, I put the small ones in one basket, the medium ones in another, and the large ones in still another basket." "Well, what is wrong with that?" "You can't imagine—decisions, decisions, decisions." Well, there's where you measure stress.

Dr. Warshaw:

There is one additional comment that needs to be made. It *is* possible to measure stress in an organization. There are a variety of indices which have been used for that. One finds, for example, a department which has a sudden increase in absenteeism and discovers after looking into it that the employees are reacting to a particular stressor—a rumor that that department is going to be closed out, or is threatened with a move, or that the supervisor of the department, a covert alcoholic, is suddenly decompensated. There are a variety of measurements (accident rates, turnover, etc.) that one can use, albeit rather grossly, to identify segments of an organization in which stress effects are somewhat higher than the norm, or are showing an upward trend. One can use such indices to identify a problem in a population segment. This is very useful to industry in deciding when and where to mount a preventive program.

Audience:

We have been reading so much about the high productivity of workers in other countries, particularly Japan. What is the major difference between their employees and ours?

Dr. Dowling:

In Japan, for instance, employees are taken on at a very early age and they are with you for life regardless of the economic situation. That would be extremely difficult in our country because of different backgrounds and aspirations, of the individual and family, different cultural values, and the fact that we live in a very pluralistic society, more so than the homogenous environment in which Japanese industry operates. There may be industries in this country which relate to their employees in a similar fashion. I am not aware of them.

Dr. Harris:

I understand from what I have read that American workers are not less productive than the workers in other countries. As a matter of fact, American productivity, as economists measure it, is still among the highest in the world. However, the rate of increase has modestly slowed or some modest decrease has been recorded, and many countries that were behind us in terms of productivity per worker, per year, have made enormous strides where we have plateaucd or moved up very little. It would be incorrect to say that any method used abroad would necessarily create greater productivity here.

Dr. Warshaw:

Higher productivity, by and large, in those countries that have developed very recently, does not reflect productivity per worker as much as it reflects new plants, new, more efficient mechanization, improved production technology. After World War II, when the factories we had bombed in West Germany had to be replaced by new ones, we gave them plants that far outstripped ours in production potential. Also, when we look at productivity among Swedish workers or German workers, we must remember that in both these countries there is an intrastructure of imported labor from the Mediterranean and North African countries. Their activities are not factored into the overall productivity. Further, if we look at some of the other countries with a highly organized work society, we discover that their rates of alcoholism, suicide, and stress-related diseases are perhaps even higher than they are in our country. So they do pay the price for industrialization.

Dr. Brahen:

About 10 years ago I had an extensive stay in Japan while visiting a number of pharmaceutical companies. I was impressed by the way the employees acted as if they were a family. Employees don't consider changing companies. Japanese employees have an allegiance to their firm and they plan to spend their life with that firm. The firm is prepared to take care of the employee from the cradle to the grave. I agree with Dr. Dowling that in Japan there is a different approach to employment.

Dr. Hammerschlag:

The Japanese workers have a unique situation and that is, they don't have a "big union" to protect them. Each one in the "family of an occupation" in Japan has got to look out for his particular group. I know a fair number of people who do business in Japan and the Japanese have a sense of pride in the quality of their production. If you produce an item and you know the item is not going to be tops, then somewhere along the line somebody is going to feel tremendous stress. Maybe the supervisor will be reprimanded or the employee will be in a poor position. This is the attitude that we have to think on.

Audience:

I have been in personnel in the health care field for almost 20 years. I find productivity in health care very hard to measure. Can you take a nurse's aide who works in a hospital and measure that she cared for 10 patients on the night shift, while another nurse's aide might have stopped and held the hand of somebody who needed comfort from pain? This happened to me when I was a patient. The guy I remember was an orderly who cradled me in his arms when I had had a spinal fusion and was in terrible pain. He stayed with me for an hour. Some supervisor must have said he wasn't very productive that night. So, if any employee is watching the clock and moving from bed to bed, is that a measure of productivity?

I have one other remark regarding stress. There are people who say that there has always been stress, but my feeling is that everybody is more aware of it now because of the media. We are exposed to it constantly. Sometimes the stressors are the people out there who make decisions for us: bureaucrats or the media. I don't let my kids watch certain television programs because the programs are too violent, but I let them watch the news and see President Reagan get shot. I told them they couldn't watch anymore of it because they showed it in slow motion, they showed it from the right arm, the left arm, and the leg. I turned it off; it was much too violent for my kids. That produced stress for me, so I turned on cable TV. They had the childhood of Adolph Hitler and my kids saw World War II. We are being bombarded by stress. We are being hit by it as never before. It is omnipresent, and I don't know what to do about it.

Dr. Harris:

Who says he doesn't know how to handle stress? That guy knows how to handle stress. He handles it with one of the best methods; humor. A sense of humor in perspective is part of the hallmark of being an adult and handling situations. However, I disagree with you in that I believe we *can* measure productivity in service organizations, including health ones. I am not a nihilist about that. Of course we can. But, if by productivity, you mean only numbers, then of course you are right. Productivity cannot be measured in a health institution as complex as a hospital or even a nursing home, by numbers alone—the number of beds made up, the number of injections, the number of bed baths— of course not. But if that number happens to be zero, I'd have to tell you that your hospital or your nursing home is in real trouble.

Of course, as Dr. Warshaw took pains to point out in his talk, the *quality* of work is as important a measure of productivity as sheer numbers. Efforts can be made to look at productivity if one incorporates measures of quality as well as quantity—not that it is easy and not that you should let the numbers go either. Numbers are not the only things that count, but they *do* count. I would say, efforts have to be made to measure the productivity in health care institutions. It can be done. *People* make stress. Except for the stress of loneliness and the occasional thunderbolt, if you were alone on a desert island, I have a feeling you would find that it was not a stressful situation. You could climb your coconut trees and take down as many or as few coconuts as you wanted. People in any social context, but especially in organizations, are the progenitors of stress.

Audience:

We have heard mentioned the stress of dual-career families, in which both the husband and wife work outside the home. More and more of us are trying to combine a full-time career with the full-time job of child-rearing. Do you have suggestions for coping with the stress that this causes?

Dr. Warshaw:

The problems are very real. Those with child-bearing, and particularly child-rearing responsibilities, indeed have dual careers. This calls for a variety of decisions to be made. Many working women have their first child in their mid-30s. This clearly reflects the decision that their careers come first and their children and family responsibilities come second. Having responsibility for children and homemaking certainly constitutes a profound stress for many people.

Organizations have attempted to find ways of handling this. One is a modified work schedule so that the parent can be home when the child comes home from school. Another one is job-sharing, in which two people share a single job. This enables them to work half-time, and while their careers sometimes advance at a slower pace, they can meet their responsibilities in the home as well. The burden of work overload, where the husband and wife both have full-time jobs and must also share the home-making responsibilities, can be a potent stressor. In many instances, it can be resolved by appropriate discussion and compromise, a kind of work "democracy" in the home. Child-care institutions provided by employers are an increasingly common answer to this problem. There are, as yet, no universal, satisfactory solutions to this potent stressor, but it is being addressed.

Audience:

My question is about numbers and money from a corporate point of view. Dr. Warshaw, you indicated that if management is properly trained, stress in the workplace will be reduced to the point where, perhaps, there will be no need for employee assistance. Should a corporation put its money toward management training or toward helping the distressed employee? Also, many distressful situations are in workplace areas that are far from mental health facilities. What is the corporations's responsibility?

Dr. Warshaw:

I don't think it is necessarily an either/or situation. Management would have to decide, in each of those instances, which they are going to do first. I would say that an employee assistance or employee counseling program can make a significant contribution. It can be installed as a formal program in which a trained counseling professional is available. In a number of instances, particularly in smaller organizations, one looks to the human resources person or the personnel manager to provide counseling capability. In instances where there is no formal counseling, there may be an older worker or a maternal/paternal type, a person to whom employees gravitate for advice. This is a very useful mechanism.

Many organizations are reluctant to institute counseling programs either because of budgeting or a lack of trained personnel. They often look to community organizations to provide counseling services. Some actually have outside counselors who are available on the premises. Others use community agencies or a private agency where employees may go with their problems. This may be paid for entirely by management, it may be contributory, it may be paid for out of the benefits, or in other ways. Those approaches all work and the choice depends on the size and capability of the organization and the willingness of managers to allocate the resources and support the program.

The preventive program, in terms of management or supervisory training, should not be aimed particularly at mental health or at stress management; it should be an intrinsic part of management. Management today has two roles. One is technical engineering: create a machine, grease it and oil it and make sure it runs properly. More important, however, is the second role of management: managing *people*. Productivity depends on people, and an essential part of management's skill is learning to work with people.

Chapter 3

LABOR LOOKS AT WORK STRESS

Melvin A. Glasser*

In recent years there has been accelerated interest in the negative effects of occupational stress. The articles in professional and scientific journals, and those in the press have identified and described the syndrome, fostered study and understanding,

*Melvin A. Glasser is director of the Committee for National Health Insurance and Consultant to the United Auto Workers International Union. During his 18 years in Detroit as director of the United Auto Worker's professional consulting staff, the union developed innovative programs in occupational health and safety, mental health, dental and vision care, and prescription drugs.

Prior to his union service, Mr. Glasser was Dean and Professor of Social Welfare at Brandeis University. He earlier held posts as Executive Vice President of the National Foundation for Infantile Paralysis and as Administrative Director of the nationwide Salk poliomyelitis vaccine field trials. Government and international service included posts as Associate Chief, U.S. Children's Bureau; Director, Mid-Century White House Conference on Children and Youth; and Administrator, International Activities, American Red Cross.

Mr. Glasser is an elected member of the Institute of Medicine, National Academy of Sciences, and former President of the National Conference on Social Welfare.

and suggested corrective approaches, some based on sound evidence, and a fair number based on creative fantasy.

It is interesting, however, that in this cascade of material, the blue-collar worker is largely bypassed. There is a great deal written about executive stress, managerial stress, the problems of doctors, lawyers, teachers, airline pilots, social workers, even professional hockey players.

Aside from one recent monograph (Shostak, 1980) and an occasional discussion piece, very few scientifically supportable studies of blue-collar stress have been conducted. Female manual workers have attracted even less interest. Though they number some twelve million, they have not attracted the interest and concern expressed for their professional and executive-suite sisters. The poor factory worker, it would appear, either doesn't have a stress problem, or has somehow learned to take care of it.

This is, of course, sheer nonsense. Blue-collar workers have major problems with stress at their jobs and in their personal lives; the pressures and possible solutions, however, are likely to be different from other social classes. It is probable that, like the field of mental health several decades ago, two phenomena have been operating: one, the assumption that generalizations about the white middle-class apply equally to the working class; two, that the values of therapists and industry management can be transposed to workers without modification.

The misleading nature of such generalization is demonstrated in a study of 23 occupations, ranging from professors to policemen, published six years ago by Robert D. Caplan, Sidney Cobb, et al. They found that assemblers and relief workers on the machine-paced assembly lines have the highest stress and strain of any of the 23 occupations. These were the workers who reported both "the most boredom and the greatest dissatisfaction with the work load." Among the factors cited as contributing to the high stress in this group were, "low utilization of one's abilities, low participation, low complexity of work, and poor person-environment fit on job complexity." (Caplan, et al., 1975)

Those who deal with illness and absenteeism in factories, attest to the facts that indicate that stress in the environment and the worker's way of coping with stress are major factors in employee functioning. The poorly functioning employee, or group of employees, is a principle factor in reduced productivity. Psychosomatic complaints, alcoholism, backpain, aspects of heart disease, hypertension, asthma, ulcers, and arthritis are some of the major illnesses believed to have a high occupational stress component. Even rate of recovery from the common cold appears to be correlated with the individual's capacity to handle job stress.

One out of every 8 workers is injured, 5,000 are killed in job-related accidents, and some 100,000 deaths related to occupational disease are reported each year. The labor-management personnel close to these situations believe personal stress plays an important causative role in the injuries and deaths. As shall be elaborated later, many believe it plays a role in occupational illness.

This has significance in terms of labor unrest. In any number of plants, a review of the hundreds and often thousands of unresolved grievances reveals that a substantial portion are often related to the handling of sick leaves and return to work. Company medical departments making decisions on the physical condition of workers and neglecting the stress factors faced at the workplace, not infrequently find resistance, confrontation, and conflict. That this contributes to labor strife and decreased productivity is therefore no great surprise.

The lack of understanding by most managements—and there are some exceptions—of stress factors affecting workers, and the frustrations of the workers with sick leave problems, account in part for worker demands for "dignity on the job." United Auto Workers (UAW) grievance machinery is replete with worker complaints about helplessness in dealing with management when the bad back diagnosed as incapacitating by the worker's physician is evaluated in opposite terms by the company doctor. The union member who persists in pressing his claim is frequently labelled, "malingerer," "malcontent," "griper." He becomes the "trouble maker" who agitates for "dignity on the job" — another way of expressing his helplessness in the face of what he considers management's intransigence.

That this problem of "dignity" is not restricted to U.S. workers is borne out by reports cited by Widick (1976). During the worker-student revolt in France in 1968, striking workers put up signs, outside their factories, bearing one word, "dignity." In Italy there was similar behavior during the "hot summer" of 1969.

Or as one U.S. management representative said to me in the early 70's, "We can give them better wages, we can offer early retirement and improved insurance, but how the hell do we offer 'dignity on the job?' " Understanding the role of occupational stress in relation to health-illness may be one of the answers. Yet, two informed observers recently wrote, " . . . most top managers and directors are generally isolated from consideration of what stress means to their companies. We do not know of a single company that has formulated a policy to manage stress. (Bensen & Allen, 1980)

In recent years we have seen greater worker sensitivity to a variety of occupational hazards. The passage of the Occupational Health and Safety Act (OSHA) in 1970 was a response to long-held worker concerns. The increase in worker anxiety, particularly in the occupational health area, is probably attributable to greatly accelerated government enforcement activities in the last four years, the development and publication of new knowledge on the hazards of substances like asbestos and other carcinogens, lead, cotton dust, vinyl chloride and other chemical intermediates, and the increased negotiating efforts and educational activities of unions and environmentalists.

The recent information that exposure to concentrations of lead in air, at then acceptable governmental standards, might cause women of child-bearing ages to have miscarriages or congenitally malformed babies, was undoubtedly stress producing. Consider the conflict of young women who are told about the health hazards of lead at their work site and face the dilemma of remaining on the job, losing their jobs, or in some instances, being offered the opportunity of transferring to other jobs at lower pay. One plant manager, seeking to be helpful, told his women workers that those who had had hysterectomies, or were prepared to have them could have the assurance of continuing job security free from worry. This major problem is still unresolved.

In a sense this is a limited aspect of the growing problems women face as they enter the work force in ever larger numbers. Their hitherto traditional roles of homemaker, primary caretaker of younger children, and their subordination to the job demands of husbands are substantially changing. However, the changes create stresses for them, as well as for their families, that are not well understood or dealt with in the work environment.

Hazard data uncovered by the United Auto Workers in the last two years that shows auto model makers, metal finishers, and other groups of workers have been experiencing up to 50 percent higher age-specific death rates due to cancer, has produced understandable workplace tension and stress. Thus far, the inability of management, the union, and government to identify the causative agents is a matter of great concern.

That these concerns are universal is evidenced by an analysis of the 1969, 1972, and 1977 "Quality of Employment Surveys" conducted for the United States Department of Labor by the Institute for Social Research of the University of Michigan. Analyzing certain aspects of production worker responses, Frenkel, Priest and Ashford reported that 78 percent of those surveyed in 1977 noted one or more safety and health hazards in the workplace compared with only 38 percent in 1969. Seventy-two percent of the men reported exposure to "fumes, dust, or other air pollution," as did 52 percent of the women. Similarly 45 percent of the men and 21 percent of the women felt themselves exposed to "dangerous chemicals." (Frenkel, et. al, 1980)

The days of the sweat shop and the Triangle fire are long since gone. Today's workers expect reasonably healthy and safe working conditions. These expectations were enhanced by the provisions of the OSHA law that require the employer to provide such working conditions. The impact of new knowledge has revealed to workers that their expectations may well be unmet.

Blue-collar occupational stress, according to Levi, (1979) "arises where discrepancies exist between occupational demands and opportunities on the one hand, and the worker's capacities, needs, and expectations on the other."

The workers' response to job stress, according to this analysis, falls into three categories:

1) Personal, emotional. This includes anxiety, depression, alienation. The steady increase in use of the UAW-employer negotiated mental health insurance benefits by auto and agricultural implement worker families in the last decade is evidence that, despite worker resistance to this type of therapy, job and personal stresses, combined with increased understanding of the causes, has resulted in greater efforts to seek relief from the negative emotional responses to stress.

2) Negative behavior. This includes alcohol and tobacco consumption, narcotics addiction, fighting, attacks on foremen and other supervisory personnel, poor quality work performance, risk-taking and self-destructive behavior. The well-known phenomenon of workers stopping off at bars for a few drinks at the end of the work shift, in part at least, can be attributed to the need to relieve tension induced by workplace stress.

3) Changes in body functions and reactions, e.g., changes in endocrine and immunological responses as a result of stress. (Levi, 1979)

Levi's analysis is useful, because when combined with an understanding of the causes of blue-collar worker stress, it provides guideposts to improved worker health through relief of occupational stress.

Principal among these guideposts are the following:

1) Increased government, employer, and union efforts to correct unhealthy and unsafe working conditions. Such efforts would not only contribute to health on the job, but would reduce the newly-induced stress of recent years that derives from improved worker knowledge of workplace hazards.

In the process of such efforts, industry and government might develop a better understanding of the newly sacrosanct shibboleths about "cost-benefit" ratios. In recent years, much of American industry has been selling the notion that safer, more healthful changes in the workplace need be made only if many people are being harmed directly and only if the changes don't cost too much.

That this concept has had such widespread acceptance is a

source of wonderment. Serious economists place a dollar value on each life potentially lost, a price on injury and incapacity, and establish cost-benefit figures on an impersonal computer. The corollary effects on the lost or injured worker's family, the costs of these losses to society as a whole, or the price fellow workers pay for the added stress experienced by working with the questionable substance or manufacturing process, don't get recorded on either the computer or the minds of those who, to paraphrase Oscar Wilde, "know the cost of everything and the value of nothing."

2) Relief from specific stress-causing workplace conditions, including excessive heat, noise, dust, odors, poor lighting, etc. Accepting the hypothesis that different individuals have different tolerance levels to adverse conditions, a visit to a foundry or steel plant in the summer months, or a stamping plant in any month, should convince even the most skeptical that adapting to stressful conditions requires using a substantial amount of that fixed, finite reservoir of adaptation energy—which Selye believes each individual possesses—needed to feed the endocrine system.

Dennis Organ reports evidence that job performance may not be adversely effected by the stress demands made upon the worker, but the involuntary "letdown," which seems necessary, may show up subsequently in poor functioning at home or in other non-job situations. (Organ, 1979) It's a vicious cycle. The lack of adjustment at home eventually reflects back on job performance and productivity, and stress management becomes increasingly difficult.

3) Redesign of difficult jobs. Numbers of production-line jobs are unduly physically stressful. Such stress could frequently be reduced through physical changes. For example, a number of auto plant assembly operations require workers to stand in pits. As the cars pass over them they work with upraised arms to install parts on the underpart of the chassis. Some companies have simply had the cars turned on their sides for this part of the operation. The workers then stand alongside the line for an operation at an arm's length level.

4) Develop worker participation in decision making. In the mass production industries, as automation increases, workers feel

increasingly frustrated as they are separated from decisions made about their tasks and working conditions. They often feel such decisions are made by managers with little knowledge of the jobs, or of the physiological and psychological price workers pay. There are hundreds of experiments now going on to give workers roles in deciding how the job should be done, under what conditions, and sometimes with what rewards. The auto industry in Sweden has perhaps made the most progress in this area. There is promise in similar projects now being conducted in the United States. Of primary importance from the perspective of our subject, this process helps reduce the workers' feelings of powerlessness and inability to influence an automated process which largely controls them.

5) Reorient company medical departments so that there is an appreciation of stress factors in the workplace. Furthermore, there is a need to separate "return to work" decisions from health protection decisions. Until this is done, workers will continue to view the medical department with hostility. This makes it exceedingly difficult to use the medical departments as referral sources for treatment of emotional disturbances, alcoholism, family problems, etc.

Finally, too many employer medical departments primarily restrict their medical activities for blue-collar workers to conducting employment medical exams, providing first aid for accidents and emergencies, and making "return to work" decisions. Far more important and useful activities should be conducted, as they are in many Western European countries.

One graphic scene comes to mind: I chanced upon a group of union blue-collar workers who were remodeling rooms to create examining stalls for a new preventive health program being made available to executives and managerial personnel of the company, but not to the factory staff. The pungency of the workers' comments, to put it mildly, indicated that their identification with their employer was not likely to be enhanced by this task.

6) Secure recognition from management of the "no man is an island" principle. Our understanding of mental health prin-

ciples has long ago convinced us that every worker must be seen as part of a family and part of a community. Accordingly, when a worker is subjected to excessive stress on the job, it often is reflected in his home situation. It is almost trite to comment that the reverse is also true.

When, in the industries with which I have been working, there was an alarming increase in narcotics addiction, an interesting phenomenon appeared. The increase was evident only in plants in those communities which were following the national trend; when the cities had no noticeable increase in the use of narcotics, neither did the plants.

Relief of excessive occupational stress therefore requires not only full protection of the worker against the costs of illness and accidents (Frenkel, et al, 1980), but identical protection for members of his or her family. This includes mental health benefits, as well as those for the treatment of substance abuse. The notion that a worker can be free from stress if he has an alcoholic spouse, or an emotionally disturbed child is of course naive. But rough estimates show that at least half of employer-provided health insurance programs do not cover dependents.

Similarly, it is of little value to provide insurance coverage for health benefits when treatment resources do not exist in the community, or community conditions are such that they nullify the curative effects of treatment.

This is not the place to discuss the employer's responsibility to the community. Suffice it to say there are substantial reasons for why the good health of the community is essential to the good health of industry and its workers.

Finally, a word about society and its effect on occupational stress. In the United States today, close to 8 million workers are unemployed. In the auto and auto supplier industries, almost one-fourth of the workers are jobless. Nationally, when 8 million people are counted as unemployed, it means close to three times that number, about 24 million people, will have lost their jobs in a 12-month-period.

From my contacts with workers I can testify that nothing, except perhaps serious illness, produces more stress in worker families than job loss, or the threat of it. In the mass-production industries in America today, such as auto, steel, rubber, and the housing and construction trades, workers are experiencing stress unlike any since the Great Depression.

The problem requires nothing short of a societal solution. The Full Employment Act of 1946 and the Humphrey-Hawkins Full Employment Act of 1978 are usually viewed as economic measures. That their purposes have not been achieved is an American tragedy. In the context of this program, job loss, or the threat of job loss, are as important a negative stress factor as any we may be considering.

REFERENCES

Bensen, H., & Allen, R. L. How much stress is too much? *Harvard Business Review*, October 1980, *58*, 92.

Caplan, R. D., Cobb, S., French, J. R., Jr., Van Harrison, R. & Pinnean, S. R., Jr. *Job demands and worker health* (Institute for Social Research, University of Michigan). Washington, D.C.: National Institute for Occupational Safety and Health, publication no. 75-160, April 1975, p. 20l.

Frenkel, R. L., Priest, W. C., & Ashford, N. A. Occupational safety and health: A report on worker perceptions. *Monthly Labor Review*, September 1980, *103*, 11-12.

Levi, L., M.D. Occupational mental health: Its monitorings, protection, and promotion. *Journal of Occupational Medicine*, January 1979, *21*, 26–27.

Organ, D. W. The meaning of stress. *Business Horizons*, June 1979, *22*, 35.

Shostak, A. B. *Blue collar stress*. Reading, Mass.: Addison-Wesley, 1980.

Widick, B. J., (Ed.). *Auto work and its discontents*. Baltimore: Md.: Johns Hopkins University Press, 1976, pp. 66–67.

Discussion

Chaired by Mr. Glasser, the panel members included: Thomas Conley, Personnel Relations, Grumman Aerospace Corporation; Audrey H. Jones, Personnel Policies and Services Manager, Long Island Lighting Company; Peter Van Putten, Jr., Director of Personnel, Hazeltine Corporation; and Charles Winick, Consultant, Central Labor Rehabilitation Council of New York, Inc.

Ms. Jones:
I would like us to look at the stress producer or stressor that the changing role of women has created, not only for women in their work and home situations, but also for men in these situations. For example, women are now back in the work force as they were during the second World War. Women today, though, have very different expectations than they did during World War II. They are not satisfied with the jobs, the salaries, the treatment that they may have tolerated years ago. Stress is caused because their expectations are not being met, and because many of them are entering the work force without the kinds of skills necessary in today's economy.

In the work situation men are also being threatened. This is because women are competing with them for jobs and in this economy, that is threatening. Whether or not women are being paid what they should is a different matter. During the war, men didn't mind women taking jobs; they were away, and when they came back the jobs were theirs again. But now if a woman gets the job, a man is *not* going to get it. This is extremely stressful for men and they are taking it out in stress-producing ways. There is still a great deal of rib-poking about women working. Often, women are called "girls," even if they are 55 years old. This has become a stress producer.

At home, there is an entirely different stress situation. There is the stress of the married woman who is trying to run a home and still hold down a full-time job. She is rushing home, doing the shopping, doing the cooking, and maybe even the dishes without much help. Her husband, on the other hand, is suddenly no longer the breadwinner of the family. Both men and women are feeling a great deal of stress.

Mr. Van Putten:

I would like to talk about stress in general. Through the centuries, stress has been a part of everyone's life. It has just become a buzzword now.

Years ago, within the work force, you were told what to do by a single, dictatorial individual who was the owner or the president, and you did it. You did your work, you were paid, and you went home and satisfied your family. There was little stress and a lot of satisfaction, because there was a good family environment.

That has all changed rapidly, particularly over the past 10 to 20 years. Our children have been taught to be more free-thinking, independent, and outspoken; whereas we, their parents, were told what to do and listened to what we were told. There have been changes in our national scene and in our international scene. The Vietnam war caused tremendous changes in what we thought and believed about ourselves and our country. The younger generation is living through a great deal of distrust—of their parents, of their country, of their world. We live in a crazy environment, and none of us knows how to deal with it because it is changing so rapidly.

If you worked hard you used to get certain kinds of benefits. Now those benefits have become expectations. We expect to have parks, we expect to have hospitals, we expect to have benefit plans, hospitalization coverage, and so on. Those things represent the security we seek, as we find there is less and less security, even in the job environment. People who have been with a company for many years may find that their company will merge with another company, the whole scene changes, and their job is gone regardless of seniority. We look for happiness, we look for security within a marriage, and we recognize that the divorce rate is close to 50 percent.

Something else we look for is more participation within the industry environment. Rather than being ordered, we want to be heard. We want self-dignity and a sense of identity. We must educate ourselves and our employees about self-awareness, to provide self-dignity, so we can fit together within an industry and work for common goals. Communication becomes more important. We communicate terribly. We think the company newspaper is the answer. We go to schools, we take courses, we try to relate to one another, but we don't do it in an in-depth way. We become very private. We are afraid of infringing on other people's rights, and the question arises, how much *can* you know about a person? How much *should* you know about a person who works for you? Do you care why they are absent, or do you just become more concerned with the pressure that is created by management saying we have got to get the project completed on time.

Our biggest resource is people. I think the problem is a lack of security—personally, on the job, and financially. This certainly produces stress. I am seeing more and more people who have stress problems on the job. The stress is not only at work, it is also outside. We are finding a greater need for psychiatric help and for the social worker. We must learn to work with each other. Management *must* realize that the environment is changing, and that we all have similar problems, including stress.

Mr. Winick:

My remarks are essentially a series of footnotes to Mr. Glasser's encyclopedic and compelling presentation this morning. From a labor point of view, I would like to talk about stress studies today, the personal dimension that is important in terms of loss of work, and the environment. We have an enormous amount of information and knowledge that is reasonably valid and current but which we are not acting on. There are journals such as *The Human Stress Journal, Environment and Behavior,* and *The Journal of Applied Behavioral Analysis* that have been published for many years, generating a substantial corpus of information available for whomever is interested. However, it is easier for society and institutions and groups to deal with the person who is in difficulty rather than to apply preventive measures to those who are at risk. In other words, it is harder to spend money now for something *not* to happen in 10 years than it is for us to spend money treating a person who already has difficulties. I think this is particularly appropriate in light of the current administration's attitude toward social problems.

I would like to underscore the effect of unemployment and losing one's work role. Toward the end of the Apollo Space Project in 1969, it was observed that the ground controllers monitoring the mission were manifesting high rates of heart attacks and other unexpected grave illnesses. Apparently, although they took great pride in what they were doing, and were proud to be part of the team that actually got men on the moon, they knew that once the Apollo's series of missions were over, they would lose their jobs. This ambivalence led to a *700 percent* increase in serious disorders.

In the 1960s when I did some studies on the effect of unemployment on the unemployed, I found that very few studies of this kind had been done since the Great Depression. I was impressed by how the unemployed people I talked to in New York were qualitatively different from other people. In order to communicate this qualitative difference, I coined a term, *atonia*, from the Greek term for lack of resonance, as in tone; when you pull a string, it doesn't reverberate. This was a much more deep-rooted sense of anomie or rootlessness or not being with it. These people, in effect, were dead. They felt dead. In many ways their emotional tone was flaccid. They felt completely unconnected after being unemployed even for several weeks. I developed a scale to quantify this and have administered it to a number of different groups around the country. Atonia was a more serious condition than anomie, which is measured by a scale developed by Leo Stole that is very widely used and is, in turn, much more serious than alienation.

In the Great Depression the studies of the unemployed found little difference between them and everybody else. At the time a lot of people were unemployed; when you compared yourself with others who were also doing badly, you didn't feel so disturbed. When a relatively small number of unemployed people compare themselves with the great majority who are working, they feel very badly about it—what sociologists call relative deprivation. In other words, it is not the explicit nature of your difficulty, but the fact that other people don't experience it that makes you feel particularly depressed.

How does the environment contribute to stress, particularly the environment related to work? Some occupations are super-high-risk in terms of stress and safety. For example, people who paint bridges have to get up on the bridge, scrape off the old paint and put on new paint. It might take eight or nine months for a crew to paint one bridge, after which it is time to start all over again. Other high stress work is done by people who handle asbestos roofing, by exterminators, by people who work with X-rays, and so on. These are only a few of the occupations with an enormously high risk of grave illnesses, especially cancer.

Most people don't work in such high-risk situations. However, even ordinary situations pose hazards that are conducive to increasing stress. As an example, noise is unpleasant and bothersome, and noise is a frequent component of many kinds of work. It increases morbidity, it decreases work effectiveness, and it has a lot of dangerous effects on the worker who is exposed to it regularly. About 40 percent of factory workers are exposed to injurious noise levels; an excess of 70 decibels. To give you some sense of comparison, 70 decibels is the sound of a light vacuum cleaner at about 15 feet.

Many work places are either too hot or too cold. Other work places have unsatisfactory ventilation. Although there have been many studies about the so-called "behavioral sink" in cities, of people being too close to one another at home, and being at an appropriate distance to shake hands and so forth, to my knowledge there is not even one good study of the effect of people working too close to one another. Yet, common sense tells us that this could have a damaging effect on work effectiveness. We must improve working conditions, because they are the single largest contributor to the workers' emotional well-being and the quality of their lives.

Mr. Conley:

Grumman Aerospace Corporation, with more than 20,000 employees, is a non-union company. First of all, we have the same stress factors as any other organization in the world. Today, we have 19-year-olds coming into the business world in entry-level jobs, and these young people are immediately faced with stress, because this is the age of instant gratification. They are in the company two weeks and they are not foremen. This produces stress. Also, when you are working in a production plant, you are in a factory, and of course, you'd rather be out in the open air, anyplace but in a factory. There is stress among some of our older people who feel strongly that opportunities for promotion have passed them by, and that they did not attain the goals they set for themselves. We have an even older group of employees who are concerned about retirement—certainly a stressful time. Change is exceptionally stressful. It occurs when a person is moved from one department to another, or from one job to another. We have, we hope, very effective communications. Is there an overall panacea in the field of communications? Absolutely not. But, we pay attention to communications in our organization. We feel that it is encumbent upon management to talk with an employee who is being moved from one job to another. Why? Because of stress. We are also beset with the other problems that all organizations have—alcoholism, drugs, divorce. We have all the stressful situations found in a small community. We have 20,000 individuals who can be subjected to stress.

Many years ago we did a survey on the needs of our people. The needs were broken down into five general areas, labeled, "Things We All Want." They were: (1) to belong: (2) recognition; (3) to know what goes on; (4) to be able to talk to the boss; and (5) to be proud of our jobs. We educate our managers, our supervisors, our foremen, to be aware of these needs, because they are personal needs. That is one way we cope with stress. We have people who are afraid to go to the boss when they have problems. A stressful situation. We have to provide outlets for that type of employee. We have problems in terms of upward mobility. Certainly, we are aware of the results of stress on our people, in terms of their effectiveness and productivity.

Audience:
    How about the experiential factor of stress? From stress you learn how to cope with additional stress. Stress has its values and, in fact, sometimes ought to be built into a training situation.

Mr. Winick:

I think there must be a distinction between dealing with a stress, and dealing with a challenge and having a successful experience. In other words, we grow and we learn and we mature by overcoming obstacles, testing our limits, and achieving successes of different kinds. However, it isn't clear that this is necessarily accompanied by anxiety or uneasiness. In other words, one can achieve without having to experience stress.

Mr. Glasser:

As to whether stress reduces or increases the ability to bear subsequent stress, there is Selye's thesis that each of us has only so much ability to bear stress, and when it is exhausted, it's gone. The individual who has a great deal of stress on the job and must contain himself and live with that stress in order to hold the job, is the one who takes it out on his spouse and kids at home. There are different views on this.

Audience:

What can the mental health industry do to teach industry about the need for mental health benefits?

Mr. Van Putten:

I don't think that industry must be educated about the needs for mental health coverage. It comes down to dollars and cents. What kind of health package can you afford? There are numerous companies that have mental health provisions within their insurance programs. You have to look at what benefits are a prime need for the majority of your employees. I think the problem within industry is that we don't really know how many of our employees would make use of that program. We must remember that we are not only insuring the employee, we are usually insuring the entire family. If the insurance is experience-rated, we might be buying a burden which could place us in a serious financial situation. That has to be considered.

Mr. Glasser:

In the United Auto Workers Union, 17 years ago, we wrote the first nationwide coverage for in-and-out-of-hospital mental health insurance. We know approximately what the use will be and what kinds of services are likely to be delivered if a specific design is included in a health insurance package covering mental health benefits. The actuaries are skilled in costing such programs. It is true that 17 years ago they told us we can't figure out who is going to use mental health services and, therefore, we can't write it. We are past that now. The problem is, what kind of coverage do you write and what services will you provide? Will you provide first-dollar coverage or will you provide economic deterrents to early detection and treatment through use of co-insurance and deductibles? Will you cover all types of therapy, or limit benefits to short-term crisis intervention programs? These are controversial areas. The costs, in fact, rarely exceed 7 percent of the cost of the medical-care package. For blue-collar workers, they run between 2 percent and 4 percent of the package. You ought to know, just for the record, that actors and actresses are probably the worst risks, and school teachers are next.

However, the question that was raised is broader than that. You want to know what can be done to encourage mental health insurance coverage. That is the responsibility of the consumers, of the groups who need the service. They should inform the insurance industry and the employers that this is what they need. Among the exceptions, to this is I.B.M., who understood the problem and told its employees, before they knew they needed it, that I.B.M. was going to provide it.

Mental health providers have, of course, been advocating such coverage for years. But their influence has been insubstantial since they stand to profit economically from a mental health benefit plan.

Audience:

I haven't heard any comment about hiring persons who, for one reason or another, have suffered emotional difficulties, who have been rehabilitated and are ready to re-enter the market place, but have certain stress limitations.

Mr. Van Putten:

Most companies have Affirmative Action plans for hiring the handicapped, and this particular category would certainly come under that jurisdiction. There are no medical restrictions to hiring individuals, other than their inability to perform a particular job. It depends on whether the skills of the individual fit the job vacancy.

Audience:

An important point made at this conference is the value of the work environment's structure in helping people feel good about themselves. Very little use is made of the available knowledge about how to make the work environment more conducive to mental health. Why are we so far behind a country like Sweden, which is looking at the relationship between worker's decision-making and the management-union fit?

Mr. Glasser:

One answer is that management-labor relationships in this country are in a different stage of development. Douglas Fraser of the United Automobile Workers is the first union leader *ever* to be on the board of a major United States corporation. We now have contractual arrangements for U.A.W. people to be on two other management boards, but that is being contested by the employers involved who question the legality of such provisions. In West Germany, by law, the workers constitute one-third or more of the membership in corporations' governing boards. Part of the reason for worker remoteness from decision-making in this country is that our industrial development still has some decades to go before it reaches the stage of most west European industrialized nations. It's a stage which recognizes that increasing productivity, quality control of products, and worker job satisfaction are enhanced by worker participation in decision making.

Audience:

We have a phenomenon called "burnout," and this phenomenon is becoming noticeable to management—employees reach a pinnacle of stress they can no longer handle. How do we handle burnout cases? Whether it is a nurse or a physician who comes in constant contact with death, a food service worker who sees clean dishes going out and dirty dishes coming back, or a porter who sees, day after day, more walls and floors to wash, burnout is a problem. I don't think we deal with those kinds of employees until the problem becomes so terrible that management can't overlook it.

Ms. Jones:

What you see as symptoms are the three A's: absenteeism, alcoholism, and accidents. We have employees who have been with us for 30 or 40 years. The movement upward has been very slow, so you do get stagnation, and job depression, which results in absenteeism, alcoholism, and accidents. What do you do about it? In the case of alcoholism, we try to get the supervisors to stop protecting. We are sponsoring programs given by the Long Island Council on Alcoholism. We try to sensitize supervisors into helping the people who have these problems to recognize them and to do something about them.

Audience:

If we deal with burnout on an individual basis, we are dealing with the bottom of the pyramid. I am living with burnout on a daily basis in the largest psychiatric hospital in New York. I have come to see it as a systemic occurrence. If we want to deal with individual helplessness, the constant change that creates this feeling of having no input, having no say, of being on a runaway horse, we have to start at the top. Badger your legislators and badger those in charge. You can only alleviate burnout on an individual basis, you can't change it.

Mr. Glasser:

I'd like to ask the audience a question, and reverse the process. Are there additional or undue stresses on women in the workplace beyond what you would expect for the average man? If there are what can be done about them?

Audience:

The answer to the first part of your question is yes. As to what can be done about it, well, Mr. Conley mentioned five things that all people want and, as I was listening, I realized that women, for the most part, don't have any of them. We must change to-kenism to commitment. That really has to be done. "To belong" was first on your list. We still live in a male-dominated society.

Mr. Glasser:

I can't go to an employer and say, "You are an employer in a male-dominated society, cut it out." We obviously have to have more specific approaches than that.

Audience:

Fine, What we need to change is attitudes. Industry needs to allow awareness programs into industry, or at least support them, so that they can be aware of why these situations are cre-ating conflict and stress within industry.

Mr. Van Putten:

I have the impression from the last comment that industries are generally not aware of the needs of their employees. That is not true. There are a lot of fine industries run by dynamic individuals who are aware of problems and are reacting to them. I hate the idea of condemning industry with respect to minorities, with respect to women, or with respect to mental health. We are working and trying hard. That is why we come to these confer-ences.

Audience:

What sense of success do you have in dealing with the stress problems that you encounter daily?

Ms. Jones:

We are trying to satisfy two of the five needs mentioned a while ago to know what is going on, and to talk to the boss. We have a program in which the president of the company, on a random basis, every two weeks, talks to about 40 different em-ployees over breakfast. They are free to ask questions and he will respond to them. If he doesn't have the answer off the top of his head, he gets back to them. This helps to bring about a better cohesive spirit between mangement and employees. We have a full-time employee counselor who is there to talk to people who have pre-retirement and retirement questions. When employees have psychosocial problems, we refer them to outside agencies.

Audience:

What happens when you make referrals and the person doesn't have the money to pay for that kind of service on the outside?

Mr. Van Putten:

We are fortunate in being in an area where there are numerous kinds of services available on a free or sliding scale basis. Companies are getting more involved in employee assistance programs, whether formalized or not, and have large listings of various agencies that are available to help employees.

Audience:

I want to pose a question that was touched on before—the "closet approach" to a problem. What do we do to break the ice? I have seen examples, not only from a business standpoint but even from a church standpoint, of when someone develops a mental problem, it is closeted.

Mr. Conley:

One of the primary things that must be done is education to create a better understanding of the problem. We need education, training, and awareness to bring these problems out in the open.

Mr. Van Putten:

It goes beyond being just an industry problem. What is being taught at colleges, high schools, and grammar schools in terms of human relationships? It has to start back there.

Mr. Winick:

Obviously not all of these problems are perceived in the same way. However, alcoholism is now relatively out in the open. In

1976, 25 famous Americans appeared in Washington and said they were all recovering alcoholics and they wanted everyone to know it. That kind of media event has a tremendous impact. Now it is more accepted. A number of famous people have admitted that they have had a schizoid episode or took lithium for depression. Mental illness is becoming more accepted. In the case, however, of other substance abuse, there are very few famous persons, who have said, "Yes, I was a heavy cocaine snorter and that is my story." That is still in the closet.

Audience:

I am president of an organization on a college campus that functions as a support and networking system for the non-traditional returning student. The majority of them are women over age 30. I'd like to add to Mr. Conley's list the need to be secure in our knowledge that we can take charge of our lives and take care of ourselves. This is what education can help to provide.

At our college we take stress and use it in a positive manner. Some of the women never finished high school, some of them had a little bit of college and then dropped out to raise their families, but now they are back and they are frustrated, and that frustration gives them stress, and through that stress, energy. We channel that energy into something profitable and productive. You don't like the job you are in, take these courses. There has got to be something out there for you. You can take care of yourself. You don't have to stay at that job. We take that and we funnel it and we channel it. Changing jobs can be challenging. It can be positive and it can be stimulating. If it is approached correctly, with sufficient training, it is positive. So, instead of dealing with all the negatives, let's take that stress and make it *work* for us.

Audience:

I work with an agency that helps the so-called "displaced homemaker"—women who are returning to the work force, the "traditional" woman. We call it the fastest growing poverty group in the United States today. This is the woman who for 30 years raised a family. This is the woman who raised the leaders of industry, who actually nurtured the children, and who now suddenly is without any means of taking care of herself. She can end up in a mental institution or in a hospital. She can end up needing charity. We are trying to put a foundation under them, trying to encourage positive thoughts about themselves, trying to give them assertiveness and awareness, and trying to get them into the work force.

But what is industry doing about new concepts of employment—flexible hours, time-sharing, or job-sharing—that may create jobs for these women, that may give them the opportunity to go to work, maybe from 8:00 to 4:00 so they can be back at home to take care of the remaining two or three children? There is something here to think about. Talk about stress, stress is the woman who raised a family for 30 or 35 years and now is age 60 or 45 or 55 without means of support.

When they tell us that women will live to be 87 years old, well, who is going to support them for the next 35 years? How do they take care of themselves? They *want* to take care of themselves.

Mr. Conley:

In terms of time-sharing, I can cite a case right in our own building. We have two sisters in our personnel office who are both married with children. They, in effect, share a full-time job. They alternate one working three days a week while the other babysits, and the other works two days a week. In certain situations this works. When women come back into industry, they experience a lot of apprehension, a lot of stress, a lot of fear. We find that as they become acclimated, their confidence level grows. It is wonderful to see a person like that succeed. We see it everyday.

Ms. Jones:

When I first started with the company, all people in entry-level jobs were young. Now people pushing the mail carts are in their 50s or 60s. We also have part-time jobs that go primarily to young women with children. They work from 10:00 to 2:00 and are home in time for the kids. We also have midnight to 6:00 A.M. shifts.

Audience:

Would it have been possible to have had a profitable panel, and maybe even this conference, without ever having used the word stress?

Mr. Winick:

Well, I guess so, since we have dealt with so many different things. The word has become, in effect, a cosmic concept, and it is also described as "future shock" as well as many other things. We have dealt with mental health, with work satisfaction, with employer-employee relations, with environmental psychology, with goals and aspirations, with levels of achievement, with minority-majority group relations, with sex relations, and with national and local politics. In other words, we have covered just about every significant area.

I think you have implied that the concept of stress is a convenient way of dealing with a large area of human and social relations.

Chapter 4

SOCIO-CULTURAL ASPECTS OF STRESS

Harold M. Visotsky, M.D.*

There is nothing new in the observation that change is stressful and that a risk accompanies every new adaptation required by an individual. By now, the work of Holmes and Rahe and their successors is familiar; life-change rating scales are accepted as reasonably accurate predictors of physical illness

*Dr. Visotsky is Owen L. Coon Professor of Psychiatry, and Chairman, Department of Psychiatry and Behavioral Sciences at Northwestern University Medical School, and Director of the Institute of Psychiatry. As Director of the Institute, he is responsible for the Department of Psychiatry of Northwestern Memorial Hospital and for the Community Mental Health Center that is an integral part of the Institute, serving a six-community area. Dr. Visotsky received his degree from the University of Illinois College of Medicine in 1951. From 1963 to 1969, he was Director of the Illinois Department of Mental Health, where he had a major role in the innovative reorganization of that department's mental health care delivery system. He is currently Vice-President of the American College of Psychiatry, and Secretary to the American Psychiatric Association. He is the author and co-author of several books and has contributed over 55 articles and book reviews to professional journals.

(Holmes & Rahe, 1967). The risk from socio-cultural change cannot be measured as directly, but its presence is undeniable. Indeed, many of the life changes that Holmes and Rahe list — a change of residence, a wife beginning to work — have socio-cultural causes. In *Future Shock*, and more recently in *The Third Wave*, Alvin Toffler has popularized the notion of a culture and its technologies evolving so rapidly that human adaptive capacity is strained to the limit and life is experienced as a series of discontinuous episodes dictated by shifting circumstances (Toffler, 1970 & 1980). We have not yet reached the grim situation of Toffler's description, but we have entered an era in which the impact of socio-cultural change is manifesting itself more and more strongly in a cynical public. More importantly for our purposes, there seems to be a disintegration of the support systems that help individuals to cope. Social change is not simply a series of events that we view through the media, but a force that is making itself felt in our medical practices.

I call this situation a crisis of battered ideals. In the past two decades, people have been bombarded by a rapid series of cultural, political, and social changes that have been experienced as intrusive, bewildering, demanding, and threatening. As a result, two interrelated crises are occurring:

1) It is becoming increasingly difficult to have settled personal aspirations in a culture where values are in a continuous upheaval, where the future is perceived as almost certain to be discontinuous with our past experiences and ideals.

2) The events of Vietnam, Watergate, Abscam and the assassination attempt have engendered an alarming degree of cynicism in which the country is seen as ungovernable, our social institutions as dysfunctional, and the business community as conspiratorial and menacing. The degree of distrust often verges on paranoia.

My contention is that the effect of so many and such rapid socio-cultural changes is synergistic. Change is taking place so quickly and in so many areas at once, that, at the same time the level of chronic stress is rising, the social integration and support that is crucial to the coping process is deteriorating.

The importance of social support as a moderator of stress

is a consistent theme in literature on the adaptive process. Close social ties are a major asset in moments of extreme stress, a source of strength that bolsters the individual's capacity or ability to cope with a crisis situation. In Detroit, a recent study of temporarily unemployed men found that those who had strong family ties or community ties, coped with job loss far better than their counterparts who lacked this support. They had fewer symptoms of illness and less of the self-blame that makes coping more difficult (Gore, 1973). A study of pregnant women found that a combined index of their life stress, on the Holmes and Rahe scale, and a measurement of their psychosocial assets provided an accurate predictor of complications in pregnancy (Nuckolls, Cassel & Kaplan, 1972).

Studies show that in a broader epidemiological perspective, people who live without family or friends, or without belonging to some supportive social group risk illnesses that include schizophrenia, multiple accidents, and tuberculosis (Mishler, 1963; Tilmann, 1949; Holmes, 1956; & Kaplan et al, 1977). Those of us who are engaged in hospital and community psychiatry are becoming increasingly aware of a core of de-institutionalized patients who wander through our urban communities forming no lasting connections with aftercare programs or other human beings. Many appear monthly — or even more frequently in some instances — at emergency rooms and crisis programs, briefly use our inpatient services, and disappear into the community until their next episode. They are one of the more extreme examples of anomie with its attendant anxiety, disorientation, and rootlessness, that Durkheim identified as characteristic of those who lack social integration (Durkheim, 1957). They are really urban migrants.

Social integration is essential to successful coping. In turn, an essential component of social integration is constancy of expectations, the sense that our environment and our fellow human beings are mostly predictable and reasonably "gratifying" (Cobb, 1976). Both constancy and gratification have a sustaining power. They allow us to envision a future, to have ambitions and goals, and, in our personal relationships, they permit us to see others in a constant role that simplifies human relationships and greatly lessens the adaptive demands of everyday life. I suppose this constancy has been undermined by the rapidity of socio-cultural change. The rate of change has accelerated so quickly and has touched so many areas of American culture that it is becoming increasingly difficult to plan, to see ourselves as living in a relatively stable environment, or to feel assured of our own place in a supportive network of human ties. You may think this isn't you, as you think about your own lives, but it represents a very significant percentage of our population. In particular, I would like to illustrate in a speculative fashion two socio-cultural factors that are having a major impact on American society and are transforming it radically: the country's current economic problems, and the emergence of new groups in the mainstream of society.

Most of the literature on economic stress deals with either the epidemiological consequences of poverty, or with crisis events that are economic, notably the effects of unemployment (Liem & Liem 1978; Brenner, 1977). A persistent double-digit inflation, and an even faster escalation of housing and energy costs are producing a more general and qualitatively different form of stress; a steady erosion of expectations for the increasing affluence that had become a staple of American middle-class society in the post-war era. Every middle-class family has measured their progress in terms of increasing affluence; if not their own affluence, at least their children's, whether through education or money. Many people are making do with less and, in the future, will have to make do with even less. This era of eroding expectations has to be contrasted with more than a generation of increasing expectations, of people planning lives that included a single-family house in the suburbs, two or more cars, regular vacations, and college for the kids.

The present attempt to modify or eliminate cost-of-living clauses is illustrative. Such a clause was a major issue in a recent strike of transit workers in Chicago, and it was during the Presidential campaign that a candidate suggested that the cost-of-living provisions in the Social Security benefits be reduced. To the individual worker, a cost-of-living clause simply means that whatever the rate of inflation, his or her wages will retain their real value. Now what employer 10 years ago would dare to suggest that employees accept a contract whose effect would be to lessen the purchasing power of their incomes over the life of their contract? How many of us, unprotected from what now seems to be the incessant deterioration of our real incomes, are being forced to cope with a once obscure fact of economics, that less really is less? The only necessary comment, since I talked about the middle-class, is that the poor are not only becoming poorer but find themselves living in a society whose commitment to helping the poverty-stricken in any material way will continue to decrease. The war on poverty is now seen as a quixotic episode in our social history, and the war on poverty is now history itself.

The stress that is arising from economic contraction can be conceptualized in two forms. The first grows out of crisis theory and identifies stress in terms of a new series of increasingly common events that arise from people having fewer options. For the middle-class, perhaps a revised Holmes and Rahe life stress scale for the 1980s will assign 10 points for each of the average number of visits per week to the gas station during the previous year. Perhaps, too, we will find ourselves defining crisis events in terms of disappointed expectations; the crisis of unaffordable housing, of not being able to live in ever-more distant suburbs; of unaffordable vacations, and the crisis of being unable to offer the next generation as much as we've had. One of the saddest things I hear when I talk to families is that, "I might not be able to give my kids even as much as I had; it is getting tougher and tougher." That is a crisis.

There is a second form of stress, a chronic rather than time-limited form, in which the frustration of unfulfilled expectations erodes confidence that our institutions and, most importantly, we ourselves, can solve problems. It would be narrow-minded to attribute the lack of confidence in social institutions solely to economics or to the divisive experiences of the Vietnam War or the trauma of Watergate. Economics touches the lives of everybody, and the stress of a long-term economic decline appears in the degree to which society's institutions are perceived as at least partially dysfunctional. The optimism that once spawned an endless series of books on how to make fortunes in the stock market, how to make a fortune in real estate, or how to make a killing in the commodity market has given way to pessimism. I stopped at Barnes and Noble where they have many "how to do it" books, and where I used to see, *How to Make a Million Dollars on Commodities.* Those books are still there, but they are selling at a discount. If you want to buy the best seller, it is *How to Prosper During the Coming Bad Years.* The author advises us to abandon big cities for small towns, to lay in a year's supply of food, to sell our stocks and to speculate in gold or high interest rates (Ruff, 1979). I don't care to argue the wisdom of these books any more than Dr. McLean did with some of the books on how to deal with stress. For my purposes, the content is less important than the underlying assumption. The underlying assumptions are that the Government will not be able to cope with inflation or will have a very difficult time, major cities are a hopeless mess, and equity investment in the future is a foolish waste of one's resources. Such a book indicates that the stress of economic change is eroding social integration. The response that put it on the best-seller list is a disquieting sign that its author's "despair" has touched broadly-felt sympathies.

The emergence of new groups into the mainstream of society is similarly breaking down expectations and threatening arrangements that were once a source of security. We are all generally familiar with the social, economic, and legal pressures to end practices that are discriminatory toward disadvantaged groups in our society. Equal opportunity legislation and affirmative action programs now provide women and minority groups with greater access to trades and professions. Both the law and the regulatory processes address themselves to the need to equalize educational opportunities, to provide greater access to housing, to make credit available. Beyond these formal changes, there is an increased visibility and aggressiveness on the part of many groups that were once hidden or passive: homosexuals, the elderly, the handicapped. Many university campuses, public buildings, and transit systems are undergoing expensive renovations in order to provide full access for the physically handicapped. Politicians have become wary of telling ethnic jokes, but it would be misleading to think of these individual actions as solutions; on the contrary, they represent the beginning of an adaptive process that will be visible at the workplace, in the educational system, in the family, and in the community at large for a generation or more. The process of role-reassessment is long term, and each new phase carries new demands and stressors. Expectations passed from generation to generation are now being upset. The first phase is militancy with its search for visibility and recognition. The stridency of this early stage is very disquieting to both the militants and the societies whose mores they have threatened. In its most extreme form, we see terrorism; its more common form is an insistence on a viewpoint that defies every effort at compromise or accommodation. We have grown accustomed to people speaking as though calling a point of view a "right" is enough to end all debate. Twenty years ago, the only visible rights movement was civil rights; now, there are women's rights, gay rights, the rights of the elderly, prisoner's rights, the rights of the mentally ill, the rights of the handicapped, the right to life, the right to choice. The stress of becoming visible is enormous, for it means not only agitating for social change but renouncing traditional role models. When a homosexual comes out of the closet and announces his or her homosexuality, when the elderly band together as Grey Panthers, when the physically handicapped stage a sit-in in a government building, they challenge both the society that has come to expect their invisibility and themselves as well. The exaggerated aggressiveness of so many of these newly-visible groups is symptomatic of their new recognition by others and their new self-image that is at odds with their own deeply-engrained cultural expectations. It is as if they have to overreact in order to change the engrained self-image.

Like militancy, tokenism carries the perils of visibility: the first woman executive in the company, the first Hispanic apprentice in the union training program, the first black family in a white suburban neighborhood. I use the word "tokenism" not as a pejorative description of the motives of the company or the motives of the community, but to portray the self-perception of any person in such a position. Militants can at least band together to provide solid support for one another, but tokenism isolates.

It places people in highly visible positions and cuts them off from their natural supports. It grants access to opportunity, but cannot grant access to the culture that is integral to that opportunity.

Consider the stress of having a job where there is little or no social acceptance outside of the workplace, a job in which one's relationships to co-workers necessarily terminate at the end of each work day. Consider the stress of the woman executive in a work culture that is overwhelmingly male, where the only other women are clerical workers who may resent her presence. Talk about role conflict, the males that she supervises resent her supervision, the female clerical workers resent her position, and she is caught in a stress bind. These are the problems that will be aggravated, not ameliorated, by job advancement. For members of the first generation to be beneficiaries of equal opportunity, each step forward will bring a new level of visibility and another level of culture that remains alien.

The increase in minorities and women in the general culture will also have an impact on that culture and will be a source of stress for the groups whose dominance is being challenged. For every group that climbs the ladder, you are challenging the dominance of the group that is already on that rung. Each opportunity taken by minorities, whether it is executive, professional, or educational, will diminish and decrease the seclusive access of others who previously laid claims to these places. Women will experience the stress of developing managerial role models for themselves, of learning to direct the activities of men who work under their supervision, and of asserting themselves in an environment that was exclusively masculine. Men will have to learn to be supervised by women, to cope with female assertiveness and ambition, and ultimately to accept that the workplace can no longer be male dominated.

Stressors caused by new groups, new positions, and new access to opportunities must be seen in terms of their interrelationship and on a longitudinal course. The magnitude of change is missed if reviewed only in a time-limited framework. The cyclical swings of the past—post-war liberalism, sexual freedom contrasted with conservative shifts in periods of distress—are changing. Mass communication and the media have impacted the changes to short transient cycles. When a change in patterns or mores begins, it is rapidly picked up by the media. Passed on to people who are not exposed to these changes, they accept them and are ready for the next change. In short, we tend to focus on competitive situations where the rules have changed. The high feelings raised by the Bakke case are examples of a situation that will repeat itself often. Many white males will find that their anticipated career paths are disrupted by affirmative action pressures, unless this government repeals everything. In industry, the once untouchable seniority system is being challenged. In any economic slump, those with special preference may be wiping out the gains of people with seniority.

It is in the interrelationship of these stresses and in their long-term consequences, that the full consequence of socio-cultural change emerges. The women's movement had its most visible impact on both the industrial and professional workplace, but it has also caused major upheavals in family life, the educational system, sexual mores, and social etiquette. It is hard to think of any major sphere of action within our culture that has not been touched by it. Our society is being forced to rethink its traditional concept of sex roles and, with the rethinking, comes the long-term stress of role ambiguity and the attendant disparity between inherited expectations and daily experience. If you think of Dr. Warshaw's comments about management stress, you see that role ambiguity, expectations, gratification, and lack of gratification are the same stressors that we have to apply over a long term to our lives. Similarly, the presence of so many new and assertive minorities demands a long-term reformulation of interpersonal relationships and roles.

The women's movement, the emergence of once silent minorities, and the radical lessening of our economic expectations illustrate social change as a stressor. The current rate of technological change also demonstrates the extreme difficulties our society is experiencing and will continue to experience in coping with a far more complex world that conforms less and less to our traditional ideas. Unlike a gradualist evolutionary model of change, the conflict between the past and present is more abrupt and, in many instances, a confrontational model. People are aware of what change implies for their future, and often, they feel powerless to influence its direction. We are witnessing a cry for simplicity that is a reaction to the stress of rapid and profound change. In political life, it takes the form of an attempt to restore traditional values or to propose extreme and simple solutions to difficult problems. The women's movement has made great advances, but the Anti-Equal Rights Amendment Coalition has also made great progress. It has blocked the ratification of ERA, even though the opposition movement only gained strength at a time when passage of ERA seemed a virtual certainty. Homosexuals are more visible in major cities than ever before, and have organized to achieve economic and political goals. However, the Anti-Gay Rights Coalition has mobilized, and in many communities has managed to prevent the passage of legislation that would guarantee equal access to housing and employment for homosexuals. In economic matters, a preference for simple solutions has gained public favor. A constitutional amendment has circulated that requires the Federal government to balance its budget. It is balancing its budget with vengeance. In my view, Proposition 13 and its sequelae represent a revolt against the powerlessness that so many people feel about declining affluence. Faced with a "revolution of declining expectations," the U.S. is becoming more conservative and traditional. The move to traditional patterns is complicated by the repudiated stereotypes, abandoned roles, perhaps discarded values. A new generation has adopted flexible attitudes and alternative life styles in place of old roles and values. I am interested in how quickly life styles change. With the move toward conservatism, toward the macho role, to frontiersmanship, we have progressed from discos to music halls playing Country Western music where people dress frontier style. I don't see many minorities wearing cowboy hats. It is almost a redneck, tough, conservative social style. Does a social style belong in a music hall? Yes, if it is pervasive.

There are other psychological responses, some of them functional, some of them dysfunctional. One of the more unfortunate byproducts of stress caused by social change has been a series of cultist panaceas that present simple prescriptions for all psychological and somatic problems. I'm sure that future anthropologists will delight in looking at the seventies and eighties as a popular culture in which low-protein diets or high protein diets, low carbohydrate diets or high carbohydrate diets, a combination of 20 different vitamins three times a day, running 15 miles a day, or six weeks in a new pseudo-pop therapy are all touted as keys to perpetual health. It doesn't matter what order you take them in as long as you take them all. It is similar to political reactions to social change. These are attempts to simplify or to present an almost mystical belief system that explains "all" and provides large paperback royalties to its originator. It is popular because it is simple.

There is also a serious and useful search for support systems that can facilitate adaptation. People are talking more about families. There has been an explosion of self-help groups with a problem-solving focus designed to provide support systems that were once more readily available in the family or the community. There are more than 500,000 self-help groups in the United States. People are searching for a common denominator, not only in coping with pathology, but in coping with a variety of life crises and chronic conditions that are either alienating or bewildering. The list of self-help populations is really impressive; alcoholics, open-heart surgery patients, compulsive gamblers, colostomy patients, mastectomy patients, the obese child, breast-feeding mothers, abusing parents, the terminally ill, psychiatric patients, single parents—there is a place for everyone. It is an interesting phenomenon because it says two things: one is that our medical and social institutions are not helping us as much as we would like them to, so we do it ourselves, and, secondly, it is a renewed linking into some kind of group phenomenon. There is a renewed interest in ethnicity even among those groups not seeking to remedy past injustices. It is a search to re-identify roots, as well as identify with the present generation.

The stress that results from socio-cultural change has major implications for my profession and yours, although any discussion of those implications must begin with two crucial qualifications. First, psychiatry has no special answers to our social problems and must avoid a global perspective that requires a solution to all the world's ills as a pre-condition for successful treatment. If everybody was rich and beautiful and happy, and had proper housing and so on, I think I could handle the psychiatric problems that remain.

Secondly, not all the consequences of socio-cultural stress are clinical. However stressful our future society, not everybody is going to be transformed into a patient, even though the risk factors will be elevated. In spite of the fact that I see you all as potential customers, you are not going to be. I'll have to live with it. Nevertheless, the implications are that for both our clinical practice as well as our social systems, we must deal with these issues not in simplistic ways. We must try and deal with them in an organized study for reducing stress in our society, and for teaching people how to cope with it. I really think you can teach people how to adapt to and cope with stress. You can't do away with stress, but you can increase the coping capacity, increase the self-esteem in individuals. We know how to do that. Not everybody is a born parent. Parenting has to be learned and increased self-esteem can be learned. We can build family ties. We can reinforce family ties. We can build surrogate family models. We can reinforce models that bring people together. Those all help coping skills and when coping skills are enhanced, stress can be managed.

REFERENCES

Brenner, H.M. Personal stability and economic security. *Social Policy* 1977, 8, 2–4.

Cobb, S. Social support as a moderator of life stress. *Psychosomatic Medicine*, 1976, *38*, 300–314.

Durkheim, E. *Suicide.* Glencoe, Ill.: The Free Press, 1957.

Gore, S. The influence of social support and related variables in ameliorating the consequences of job loss. (Doctoral dissertation, University of Pennsylvania, 1973).

Holmes, T. Multidiscipline study of tuberculosis. In P.J. Sparer (Ed.), *Personality stress and tuberculosis.* New York: International University Press, 1956.

Holmes, T. H., & Rahe, R. H. The social readjustment rating scale. *Journal of Psychosomatic Research*, 1967, *11*, 213–218.

Kaplan, B. H., Cassel, J. C., & Gore, S. Social support and health. *Medical Care*, 1977, *15*, 47–58.

Liem, R., Liem, J. Social class and mental illness reconsidered: the role of economic stress and social support. *Journal of Health and Social Behavior*, 1978, *19*, 139–156.

Mishler, E. G., & Scotch, N. A. Sociocultural factors in the epidemiology of schizophrenia. *Psychiatry*, 1963, *26*, 315–343.

Nuckolls, K. B., Cassel, J., & Kaplan, B. H.. Psychosocial assets, life crisis and the prognosis of pregnancy. *American Journal of Epidemiology*, 1972, *95*, 431–441.

Ruff, H. J. *How to prosper during the coming bad years.* New York: Times Books, 1979.

Tilmann, W. A., & Hobbs, C. E. The accident-prone automobile driver. *American Journal of Psychiatry*, 1949, *106*, 321–331.

Toffler, A. *Future shock.* New York: Random House, 1970.

Toffler, A. *The third wave.* New York: Morrow, 1980.

DISCUSSION

Participants in this discussion, chaired by Dr. Visotsky, were: Fred B. Charatan, M.D., Chief of Psychiatry, Jewish Institute of Geriatric Care; Rosemary Lukton, D.S.W., Professor, School of Social Work, Adelphi University; Michael J. Petrizzi, C.S.W., Director, Nassau County Administration, Diocese of Rockville Centre, Catholic Charities; Maurice S. Satin, Ph.D., Assistant Director, Division of Mental Health Care Systems, Long Island Research Institute, New York State Office of Mental Health; and Isidore Shapiro, A.C.S.W., Commissioner, Nassau County Department of Mental Health.

Mr. Petrizzi:
While I would like to say that where I work, everything is great and that we allow staff to get involved in decision making,

this isn't really true. Very few places will help to increase staff morale and lessen stress by allowing employees to make decisions. I do feel, however, that an alternative to this is sharing decisions with people, calling them in, letting them know why you are doing what you are doing. Obviously, the goals of your staff should be the goals of your agency and there should be a meeting of the minds. I certainly agree that people should get feedback and understand what is going on so that they don't feel isolated on the job. I also feel very strongly about letting staff members know how well they are doing.

Dr. Lukton:

I think I would place a slightly different emphasis on the data that Dr. Visotsky marshalled, although I am basically in agreement. I would emphasize less the rapidity of change that we are now experiencing. I think that, in this country, we have always undergone rapid socio-cultural change; I am not sure that the stress we endure now is any greater than the stress of crossing the plains in a covered wagon. I don't know that the isolation we endure in this century is any greater than the isolation of residing in a sod hut in South Dakota in the last century. The rapid change that followed the mass production of the automobile and the sequela of World War I probably occasioned just as great a demand for changing roles as the E.R.A. will ever do.

I believe our real emphasis should be on what we can do to develop new networks for supporting people as they endure change. The breakdown of the family and religion makes support systems much more necessary. We are all aware of the self-help movement, and it seems that if the supports are not there, they have to be invented, and people will invent them. As professionals, we may find ways of helping that process.

Dr. Satin:

I am a sociologist by training and an epidemiologist by practice. From these points of view, physicians deal with the effects stress has on our bodies. Psychologists can teach us how to deal with the stresses that we encounter. But interventions leading to the *primary* prevention of stress are best aimed at the socio-cultural environment.

Most of the potential areas of intervention were covered by Dr. Visotsky. My interpretation lies somewhere between the hypothesis that says accelerated change is responsible, and the hypothesis that says we are dealing with a breakdown of social supports. Perhaps we can learn how to integrate these two approaches for our benefit by using some of the oriental models of work productivity which build social supports into the workplace. To use people's time effectively in this regard, the one-third or more of their lives they spend at work might profitably be a source of social support. Such a situation would change the way people perceive and deal with stress and could result in increased productivity in the workplace.

Dr. Charatan:

The importance of stress as a factor in psychiatric disorders is reflected in Axis 4 of the Diagnostic and Statistical Manual (DSM III) of the American Psychiatric Association. This axis rates the severity of so-called psychosocial stressors on a scale from one or "none," to seven or "catastrophic." Among adult examples given as illustrations are: under three or "mild," argument with neighbor; under four or "moderate," new career; under five or "severe" is listed a major financial loss. Conspicuous by its absence from this list is work stress.

Any experienced psychiatrist or counselor knows that most work stress has two main causes. The first cause is an interpersonal problem. The second is time pressure, the need to meet a deadline set by one's boss. Let me briefly consider stress arising from interpersonal conflicts at work. There are some basics which must be accepted by those trying to treat work stress that interferes with productivity.

First of all, it is inescapable that political relationships exist in any work situation. Every organization contains a hierarchy as well as official and unofficial pathways of power and influence. Second, anyone who experiences stress at work needs to know that he or she is not alone, that co-workers, subordinates, and supervisors are also affected. Thus, group counseling has an important role in reducing stress, not just for the individual, but for the entire organization. If one can reduce the total amount of stress within the organization, one helps each worker. This is because stress is cumulative and interactive according to the system's viewpoint. Third, it is important for the counselor to foster respect for co-workers and supervisors as well as subordinates, even in situations where liking others has become difficult if not impossible. This is particularly important where there is a need to discipline, criticize, or disagree. It is always worth recalling the useful old saying that one can disagree without being disagreeable.

Finally, we have to get away from the overly simplistic notion that the individual deals with stress through flight, fright, or freeze. This may be appropriate for animals, but people can react in another way which is being much written about. This is the so-called "burnout" syndrome. By this we mean a partial or complete disengagement from work; a kind of secret, internal, psychological flight resulting in lowered efficiency and morale and high turnover. Unfortunately, burnout affects more managers, supervisors, and others in positions of responsibility than it does the rank and file. It correlates rather highly, as I am sure you know, with alcoholism, mental illness, marital conflict, and suicide.

I need hardly say that some stress is essential as a spur to everyone in an organization. But we, as mental health professionals, seek to recognize the danger signals of excessive stress and help management deal with it before it affects productivity.

Mr. Shapiro:
One of the things that impresses me is the general tendency to simplify everything and reject complexity. It seems that the development of self-help groups is an attempt to make things so narrow that everyone can find a ready answer to problems that are really much more difficult to solve than we are willing to accept. Dr. Visotsky mentioned that there are 500,000 self-help groups. That is a lot of groups. Perhaps we can talk about why so many of the groups that spring up are really negative groups. They are opposing not affirming something. I don't

know if this is a quality that has come up in our time, or whether it has existed throughout history.

Dr. Visotsky:

Unless you talk about stress in the light of coping, you are merely talking about problems. We could spend days listing the stressors, either individually or collectively. There is a kind of paradigm for coping; in expressing coping as an equation, the denominator would be the constitutional basis, the genetic makeup (what is called susceptibility), plus the stresses and stressors under the enumerator which is self-esteem, plus support systems. We know that self-esteem and support systems are effective ways of dealing with the crises, the stresses, and the stressors. That is what coping is all about. Not whether you *get* into crisis but whether you can *recover* from crisis. Not whether you are *exposed* to stress, but whether you can effectively *manage* stress.

$$\text{Coping \& Adaptation} = \frac{\text{self-esteem} + \text{support systems}}{\text{constitutional make-up} + \text{genetic factors}}$$

I agree that the stresses and strains of crossing the plains were indeed great, but I consider that to be the original "outward bound" system, which is a great technique for learning to deal with stress. It is the training for proper levels of dependency among individuals, for working in unison to overcome the stresses and strains of the environment, and for getting to a common goal. It is slightly different from feeling alienated.

Audience:

I am a psychiatrist in private practice. What is the one important constant in human existence? *Change* is the only constant in human experience. How have we taught our children to cope with change as it occurs from day to day? The planet we live on is not constant. It changes from second to second—plate movements, earthquakes, volcanoes, floods. We have to learn to cope with it.

Audience:

Many well-meaning physicians are prescribing mood-altering chemicals for handling stress, but very ofen these chemicals compound the problem.

Dr. Visotsky:

The most common prescription for what seems to be a stressful situation, mostly among the poor, has been Valium. Frequently, patients are hustled out without a chance to really talk. On one hand, we say talk to a friend, talk to a minister, talk to a doctor, talk to someone about your problems and, maybe by ventilating, you'll get a series of alternatives to deal with the stresses in your life. Instead, some get a prescription which either puts them into mild depression or deepens whatever problems they have.

Audience:

When there is a death in a family, which we would call a part of life, very often the very first thing that happens, as soon as that death certificate is signed, is the prescription that denies us the grief experience.

Mr. Shapiro:

As I said earlier, we attempt to simplify things that are very complicated. Death is an extremely complicated experience. Not only are drugs prescribed, but people want them, indeed expect the doctor to prescribe them. A pervading notion in our country is that we ought not to experience any pain, even though pain is an inevitable feature of life. The capacity or the willingness to confront that we *do* experience pain, helps us grow and develop our increasing capacity to deal with stress.

Dr. Lukton:

We know a great deal now about the stages necessary to resolve mourning. Professionals are learning the predictable phases of resolution, of crises that develop; crisis intervention is a positive contribution that we can make.

Mr. Shapiro:

Crisis intervention is a new phrase that springs from the mental health field. We are always intervening in crisis. Of course it is true that one should respond to crisis; however, let us not institutionalize crisis intervention. A proposal was made to me recently to form a response group that would run and offer help whenever there is a death. I felt that it was a rather grotesque proposal. It is hard enough that people have to deal with death without someone intruding, asking, do you want me to help you? What seems to be lacking in our culture are some of the ordinary responses from people around you: your family, your friends. This lack, which is creating some of that change in our culture, is what we have to reorient ourselves to recreate. I would not like to see it bureaucratized—having a system of specialized people doing all these little things that people should do for one another.

Dr. Visotsky:

It is not beyond us to go back to the educational model; to let people understand what grief and mourning are all about. It is OK to cry, it is OK to put your arms around someone, it is OK to hold someone. We really don't educate people to do that, and I think that is a very important part of education. It's not complex. It is not unreasonable to demand we learn that. I don't know why we can't expect that people understand the simple mechanisms of individual reactions. I think that we have not expected as much as we should from each other.

Audience:

We seem to constantly go from brush fire to brush fire. We talk about the alcoholic employee, we talk about drug abuse, we talk about the maladapted employee; in other words, we talk about the problems and not the solutions. I would like to see a model established that we could take back into our production area and say, "this is something we should be doing." I would like to take back a philosophical approach, a teaching approach; as far as stress and its relationship to productivity is concerned, we don't seem to have any models.

Mr. Shapiro:

A working model starts with the premise that those of us in any positions, especially leadership positions, ought to be concerned about and responsive to the people we work with; responsive to them in a genuine way, not as a device or a mask, but as something that you feel responsible for, have an interest in, and take the time to follow through on. That kind of attitude in working places would change behavior.

Dr. Charatan:

Much has been said about the importance of open communication. In any organization, whether it's a corporation or a service organization, group process and group discussion is the key; together, of course, with individual counseling and discussion of the handling and understanding of stress. In our democracy, open-mindedness and informality are the keys to success. From what we read and hear about behind the Iron Curtain, where essentially they have a paranoid society, the problem of alcoholism has become enormous, but concealed.

Audience:

I am a hospital personnel director. This thing we in management talk about—encouraging open discussion in the workplace—is a lie put into employee handbooks to impress the outside world. This lie is used in the health field. As an example, when an evaluation form from a patient who is leaving the hospital is very critical of the hospital stay, the administrator says, throw it out, he must be some sort of crank. But when they get a good letter, they publish that in the employee newsletter. Industry does this too, and so do hotels. They have little post cards on the night tables that say, how did you enjoy your stay, what would you do to improve it? I fill out the cards conscientiously, but nothing is ever changed or corrected.

When we recruit, we say we want bright young people to fill challenging jobs in stimulating careers. Do you know how many bright young people are destroyed in organizations because they come in with ideas that are going to rock the boat? What is causing a lot of stress in the workplace is that by the time you find out what has caused the stress, the employee has already done one of two things: he or she has either gotten fired, or has resigned.

Then you go through the nonsense of the exit interview, another big lie. The form that the person is asked to fill out asks, what didn't you like, what did you like, how did you like your supervisor, and so on. Who would *dare,* knowing the reference checking systems, fill that out in an honest way? Who is going to write the truth? I've never met an employee who felt comfortable about an exit interview. We encourage this honesty on the surface, and at the same time we stifle it. I've tried other methods. I use a post-exit interview. When people leave your workplace and are gone for six months, they might be more inclined to tell you, by mail, what they really think.

I would venture to say that if you go into any institution, any factory, any business, any hospital, to talk to employees to find out what they are really thinking, you'll find that most of the time they will tell you what management wants to hear. I would appreciate some comments about openness because I don't think it exists.

Dr. Visotsky:

One of the problems with open communication, whether it is phony or not, has to do with one word that we have forgotten. Dignity. Don't promise anyone anything if you are not prepared to deliver on the promises. Phoniness arises when you make your employee swallow something that you don't really mean. There are exit interviews that are useful. They are not written, and they are based on some kind of communication standard which has to do with the dignity of the individual. To ask routine questions and say, "we are going to have an open communication meeting," is undignified, because it doesn't respect the right of the individual to be comfortable in the communication process.

If the purpose of communication has to do with improving the system legitimately—not just for cataloging knowledge or filling out forms—I think people will learn how to communicate. It is tough and most of it is phony. I must agree with that.

Mr. Shapiro:

Open communication implies a free-for-all statement. There is another word we should keep in mind—tact. One has to ask questions that are appropriate to the situation. In the exit interview, if you are really genuine about it, you are trying to learn something about the person's feelings, appreciating the fact that he or she will not tell you everything. Any sensible person knows that when you don't have enough connection to another person, it is not intelligent to be as candid as a child is. Civilized society requires you to make judgments as to what you say.

Dr. Charatan:

To underscore what Dr. Visotsky said, one aspect of improving openness is certainly to improve the system, and, in psychoanalytic terms, perhaps that means decreasing the resistances of both suppression and repression. I will quote an anecdote about suppression and repression which may illustrate what I mean. A British soldier is being brought back from the great retreat at Dunkirk. His uniform is in tatters, and he has lost all his gear and weapons. As he gets off the boat, there are several reporters waiting to interview him. One of them asks, "Tell me, what was it like there?" The soldier thinks for a moment, and says, "Well, not too bad, but the *noise* and the *people.*"

Audience:

I would like to relate the comments on self-esteem and dignity to the comments about the number of groups that are coming out and *de facto* announcing their rights in a way that prohibits or stops discussion. Also, in our desire to give people their "rights," sometimes we put them into positions they are unqualified for, and that causes stress. What might be a better system?

Dr. Visotsky:

Many of these issues must be seen in a multi-dimensional system like a matrix. Although you may be trying to provide equal rights, at the same time you isolate those individuals, either because they may not have the proper experience, but have potential and are isolated from their own peer group, or because they stand alien. These stresses are part of the developmental processes. They are the crossing of the plains, to get to the other side. You really have to be put through them. There are no shortcuts. The stridency and militancy you hear, really come from being unsure. As you hear yourself shouting and talking you become more confident and then someone else joins you. It is an evolutional process for gaining power. Nobody gives you power, you have to take it. Although you may be given opportunities, only when you really begin to move and to use power do you have it.

Audience:

I have known a few people who did not take a promotion in order to remain within a peer group, to avoid isolation and remain at a comfortable level. They were actually working at odds.

Dr. Visotsky:

In the late 1950s we studied production at a large appliance factory. We stood at the gate and asked, "What do you do?" They would say: "I'm an electrician," or "I'm a machinist." Some 20 years later, at the same factory, when we stood at the same gate and asked people what they did, they said, "I work on the assembly line." "What do you do on the assembly line?" "Well, I wire things." "What would you call yourself?" "I'm an electrician." It is an interesting phenomenon in that it involves a person's loss of esteem for their ability as an expert or a worker. That company began to insist that people who worked with electrical things be called electricians. They didn't promote them, but they used a kind of matrix system in which you didn't have a number of supervisors, but had expert leaders who were really electricians or machinists, and so on. Their production went up. First you built self-esteem by not letting them say they worked on an assembly line; you insisted that they identify with a particular craft, and secondly, you allowed the leadership to remain intact within the group.

When the workers were asked if they thought the system would continue to work, their response was: we don't care if it works or not; the important thing is that they are trying to work *with* us. That is imporant and we didn't have to use labor clout to do it. It came out of some ideas we had. Labor clout to them wasn't as good as their involvement .

Mr. Shapiro:

Those of you who have studied music know that in order to learn a piece, whatever your instrument, you always try to play something a little bit beyond your capacity. People ought to have an opportunity to try things a little beyond their scope. Of course, people in a place want to keep that place and don't want new people to move into it. I think that is inevitable in social relationships, and to say that we should eliminate it is really flying in the face of human behavior. As Dr. Visotsky said, the atmosphere or milieu is very important; changes should be made out of respect for people's dignity and possibilities, not for what they do at the given moment.

Audience:

I am a social worker. My concern is that we are in an ice age, culturally and professionally. We are afraid to touch people under stress because it is not "professional."

Dr. Visotsky:

For years we used a cookbook approach. One psychiatrist advocated taking the patient on your lap and cuddling him; another believed in swearing at the patient. Somehow we can't build a repertoire of skills for the helping professionals in which we can act appropriately to the situation and to the time. Yes, it is appropriate to put your arms around somebody if they are in grief or they are in stress or they need someone to keep them from running—not physically, but mentally. There are times when you must very strongly tell a person to sit down and pull themselves together. There is no *one* brand of therapy. We must learn a repertoire of roles, each appropriate to the specific setting.

Audience:

In industry, where there is a lot of stress and stress reactions, would industry profit by having a resident psychiatrist who could institute group therapy with any group of workers who demonstrated excessive degrees of work anxiety?

Dr. Visotsky:

Stress is not always evident at the work site. We may get *results* of stress. Absenteeism is a manifestation of stress as are poor productivity and poor workmanship. You won't see people break down and cry very often. They go *home* and break down and cry. They go *home* and punch the kids. That is why I don't think group therapy will work in a job setting. What is important, however, is to get companies to take some responsibility for their employees, to offer them time to think and to learn, and to see the work site not as a place that only creates stress, but to understand that stress is transportable; you take it with you.

Mr. Petrizzi;

In our work in Catholic Charities we receive many referrals all men and women who are having difficulties adjusting on the job. All social agencies, obviously, have these referrals. We *are* getting those cases for counseling and for treatment. They are not coming by way of the plant or the office, they are coming on their own.

Audience:

I am an administrator in the public school system. The denominators of self-esteem and dignity seem to be one way of dealing with stress. The larger that denominator the lower the distress. Yet, it seems that contracts and unions diminish the supervisors' ability to deal with the self-esteem and dignity of the individual. A worker applies for a personal day; the contract says he must give a reason for it. The supervisor must deny that personal day unless the worker specifies the reason. The contract says three days for death in the family. The worker is traumatized and needs six days. How do you deal with the constraints and restraints of due process and contracts and still respect self-esteem and dignity?

Dr. Visotsky:

Those are very difficult issues. There are a couple of companies that do not ask the employee to explain the reason for a personal day. It is a *personal* day. It could be picking flowers or walking in the sun. One company increased the personal days for both middle-range and top-range executives to 12 days a year, which was a programmed response to some of their stress. Most executives didn't use any more than six or seven, partly because of their own anxiety and competitiveness—if they are away too long, people would think there was something wrong with them. But interestingly enough, top management actually did see a reduction of stress so they increased it to 15 days. Even though not even the 12 days were used, they increased it to 15 days to allow executives a greater latitude, knowing that when you take some time off in the middle of the week and you walk away from your desk, you come back better.

We know from other stress research that people who work on computers—especially key punch operators and word processors—are now one of the largest stress groups. They are even higher than air traffic controllers. They are stressed because the machines are usually put in rooms where there is a lot of light, so eyestrain occurs. If you give them 15 minutes off each hour, their productivity goes up 25 percent. But they don't have 15 minutes off each hour. They have 15 or 20 minutes every three or four hours, and their productivity goes down. Only a few companies allow these employees to take hourly breaks, others think it is going to set a precedent for other clerical workers. That is unfortunate.

I think we can teach industry and labor unions how to use their contracts in terms of lifestyle rather than as points on a Brownie scale.

Audience:

Have you found that adherence to the work ethic—working hard versus hardly working—causes any stress?

Dr. Satin:

Any consideration of the socio-cultural origins of stress in this society involves a discrepancy between the expectations that society presents to people in specific roles and the means that society gives them to fulfill those expectations. Take, as a generalized example, older workers who were taught a strict work ethic, versus younger workers whose value system says maximize my immediate return. I am not stating these as absolutes; there are exceptions. But indeed when workers wanting to maximize their immediate return are supervised by people who believe in the individual doing a good job for its own reward, there are bound to be conflicts. That value conflict is certainly a socio-cultural basis of stress in the work place.

Most highly affected by occupational stress is the middle manager; the person responsible for meeting the demands of the top echelon at the same time he or she is trying to increase productivity. They are caught between a rock and a hard place. Many of the fundamental background issues in this kind of stress sandwich, if you will, are differing value systems. We do not inculcate the work ethic. The work ethic may, in fact, be a passé approach to productivity. In fact, doing a job for the job's sake is not the underlying ethic in many productive work environments.

Audience:

I am a clergyman. I'd like to illustrate what we've been discussing by a story. Three men were working with wheelbarrows and stones and cement. A passerby came along and asked the first man, "What are you doing?" He answered, "I am chipping stone." The passerby asked the second man, "And what are you doing?" He answered, "I am building a wall." When he asked the third man "What are you doing?" the man said, with pride, "I am building a cathedral." This ties in with the value structure we have been talking about.

A person enters his work experience with personal attitudes, and maybe some pride. Some people do not bring pride to the workplace. Others may lose it sometime during their working years. Maybe that loss of pride comes because of lack of communication—the boss doesn't know how the worker feels. Are there any guides to help the top level really know and feel what the mass of workers is feeling?

Mr. Petrizzi:

I am responsible for 100 employees. In the hiring process, I have personally interviewed close to 80. Part of the interviewing technique, of course, is to explain in full detail the job requirements and the goals. We discuss this at some length. If the person is suited for the work that we have in mind, we come up with an agreement, a contract. We will offer a certain salary if he or she feels that they can perform this task. That is number one. When we confirm the employment, we put into writing the conditions of employment. Employees are also given a personnel policies manual, containing policies such as personal business days, days for funerals, etc. Now, during employment, if more days are needed, then they can appeal to the director. There can be exceptions. In other words, the individual knows who the "boss" is and that individual has a right to ask for an interview or for a meeting. Another goal is, of course, to make myself visible, to be at each office, to let them see me, and to be available for all confidential interviews. We do not feel that this is in any way undermining the authority of the supervisor.

Audience:

What about executive stress? Who takes care of the person at the top who has to take care of and meet all the needs of others? Is his power enough to sustain him?

Dr. Visotsky:

It used to be that executive stress was diminished by the privileges, the fringes, if you will, consistent with large corporations. But those fringes are being attacked now, so that his car is assessed against his taxes, his plane is assessed against his taxes, and so on. The executive still has the latitude of power. I don't mean absolute power, but the fact that he can set up objectives within certain reasonable areas for himself. We used to think that the person on the top had all the pressures because the buck stopped there. However, it is the middleman who gets squeezed.

Audience:

Because the ordinary worker in any office or workplace is always surrounded by people, controlling stress is very difficult.

A corporate manager has a private office; he can close his door. He can relax and shed frustration and anxiety. The ordinary worker can't. This causes a difference in their levels of stress.

Dr. Visotsky:
   Many corporate presidents have been moved out of their own offices. Some 200 corporation presidents have been replaced in the last three years. Fired. That was frowned upon until now. You saw them move out or retire only when they *wanted* to move, but now boards are firing presidents. Life is not a bed of roses for corporate presidential expectations. The president who felt he had his job for life, but who gets fired in three years, is under the same kind of stress, relative to his expectations, as someone in another position. I am not quite sure that the top executive has the same level of stress, but we are not matching levels of stress. Stress is based on the perception of the individual. If I am in a stressful situation and I don't perceive it as such, then I am not stressed.

Mr. Petrizzi:
   Some of the studies on executive stress highlight that many executives that we expect to have heart attacks do not because they know how to handle their stress. Many executives succeeded because they are tough. Of course the opportunity to delegate helps.

Dr. Satin:
   I agree that stress is stress. Whether you look at the outcome of stress in terms of physical health, mental health, or social competency, the people who have the poorest health in this country, mentally and physically, and the people who are the least socially competent, are the poor. If one wants to find where the impact of stress is greatest, we know where to look.

Audience:
   I am a Roman Catholic priest. We are not looking at the real meaning of man, the real meaning of our existence. This is why we can throw out executives and fire the assembly-line worker. We have to find out how we can restore a meaningful

life to people. We keep mentioning life styles; I haven't heard life's *meaning*. Not one person has said anything about the essential roots, the very fiber, the very center of our lives. We need more solid things than the many myths I have been hearing, reinforcing us with laughter, anecdotes, and jokes. I don't think we have penetrated the meaning of what is happening to us. Yes, we run from brush fire to brush fire. Just when we think we have it put out, the volcano explodes again. I have read no surveys about our perceptions of the meaning of life.

Dr. Satin:

We do have a survey about what the meaning of man's life should be in this country. We have it every four years. It is called the general election. The 1980 election, probably more than any since slavery days, has made a clear statement about what the majority wishes man's meaning to be, at least for the next four years. In order to live with that, I think we have to educate our fellow man in conjunction with whatever social resources we can muster, because if we are to believe the political rhetoric, the meaning of life in the United States is every man for himself and the devil take the hindmost.

Audience:

There is now an array of books, like *Winning Through Intimidation, Power,* and so on, about how to put other people under stress. Our country is loaded with books about how to defend yourself and trip the other guy.

In *Power,* Michael Korda tells how to rearrange your office so that you look bigger and make the other guy uncomfortable. If you want to cut a meeting short, turn off the air conditioning. It is about how to do your fellow man in. So, too, humanity is often lost in big corporations and in labor-management relationships when things get hot.

I agree with the school administrator that contracts often take the humanity out of proceedings. What if you were brought up by a woman who was not even a stepmother, but who loved you and took care of you. When she dies, you don't deserve three days?

As a personnel director, I deal with benefit programs. The

programs—not just mine, all of them—are counter-productive regarding the area of stress and productivity. Most of them will pay 80 percent if you have a good solid coronary or a good bleeding ulcer, but for a stress-related disease, they pay 50 percent. Those who provide the benefits—some of the biggest businesses in America—arbitrarily set a fee schedule that prevents people from seeking help until they get the coronary.

Dr. Visotsky:

The insurance marketing people will say that if they gave you a list of diseases for which you wanted to be insured and you rated them from one to 50, you would put heart attack and cancer first, and stress would be last.

Audience:

I am a high school principal. As we have been talking, I sense that the level of distress in the room is rising. I am wondering, if you, as members of the panel, are feeling that and I wonder what you attribute that to?

Dr. Visotsky:

Yes, I have been feeling it. I am not sure what I can attribute it to, except for two things. One is that we have been sitting for a long time. That is distressful. Secondly, we have all said it, there are no single answers to these very complex questions. You've expended our expertise to give you that magical answer. So we are going in circles. You had questions ranging from the systems operation to the most theological operation. I think we need both. And the answer is, we don't have all the answers.

We can point your own lives in some direction and show you those systems which have power to bring about change. For those systems, I would just ask you to think about how you can make that change within yourself, what you need to learn, and what you have to teach others. You came here as helping professionals, and you have to decide how to help others and how to help yourself.

You can't do it all tomorrow. In fact, maybe for the next couple of years it will be very difficult to do. It is not money alone. It is commitment to a valuable ideal.

Chapter 5

STRESS—HOW USEFUL A CONCEPT?

Joseph N. Ruocco, Ph. D.*

The first idea that I would like to discuss is "labeling."
Webster defines the word "label" as a term or phrase "attached
by way of classification or characterization, to affix a label, to
mark with a name, to describe or designate by a label, to tag."
We use words to describe and communicate our ideas and our
feelings. We label our feelings and our ideas with words, and

---

*Dr. Ruocco has more than 25 years of academic and industrial
experience. He contributed to leadership research projects while a
member of the armed forces. He has headed a Life Sciences Research
Group at the New York University College of Engineering. He headed
a similar group at Grumman Aerospace Corporation before joining their
Personnel function as a Manager of Personnel Development. He joined
I.T.T. where he was a Personnel and Administration Executive for more
than 10 years. He has had extensive experience in management consulting, executive performance review, and executive assessments. Dr.
Ruocco, a graduate of Fordham University with a Ph.D. in Psychology,
has held Adjunct Professorships at Marymount Manhattan College and
Adelphi University. He is presently Assistant Professor at Adelphi University's School of Management Science and maintains a private practice
specializing in executive assessment and counseling.

after a time the words come to equal the ideas or our feelings. I submit that we don't reflect enough on how inadequate that process is, how powerful it is, how devastating it can be, how useful, how misleading, how much a part of our fabric it is. I am not dealing with anything new. Every major school of philosophy has dealt with, and continues to deal with the problem. Nominalists pretend to resolve the problem by denying its existence; indeed by insisting that the word is the idea and that no distinction really exists between the thing and the word, between the idea and the word used to express it.

The social philospher, Hobbes, once wisely observed that the power of society lies in the fact that it can assign labels to people and then enforce their definition. Consider that for a moment: the tremendous influence and power that society wields over us because of grossly oversimplified labels that it can assign. "College graduate" is a label that society allows us to wear if we go through a prescribed ritual, at a state-approved institution, which culminates in a rectangular piece of paper which states "Bachelor of Something." Most of us don't understand the meaning or the etymology of the word bachelor in that sense. Often in the past the piece of paper was written in Latin. We didn't even know what it said, but we dedicated four years to the pursuit of that piece of paper. A large segment of our society feels bad indeed, and pays a substantive economic as well as psychological price because they are not permitted to label themselves "college graduates." What about all the other societally-sanctioned labels that carry prestige and feelings of adequacy and achievement or that carry ineptitude and feelings of failure and unworthiness, and all of the blander labels in between. Consider a few: felon, doctor, ambassador, student, handicapped, minority, Nobel Laureate, prostitute. We summarize a whole life with a simple label. What about all the other labels that we, learning from society, assign to ourselves and others? What about the role labels that we use? Father, wife, husband, child, mother, lover, laborer, Jewish, Protestant, Catholic, American. How about the competency labels that we assign? Bright, stupid, handsome, ugly, lazy, energetic, strong, weak. What I am trying to say is that words originally intended to describe something about reality can easily take on a reality of their own. They gradually cease describing and being dependent upon the reality that prompted them, and become ends in themselves. They assume what we psychologists call a functional autonomy, a life of their own.

All of us here are directly or indirectly involved with a field that contributes much to this state of affairs. In trying to better understand people we attach all-subsuming labels to them: character defect, anxiety neurotic, schizophrenic, hypochondriac, psychotic. And we attach over-simplified labels to explain the causes of the problems.

To be sure, "stress" is just such a word. It is on everyone's mind today. It is a sloppy term, widely used and widely misunderstood. However, it has also served some potentially useful ends. More than any other single word, "stress" has spawned a whole new professional discipline called "behavioral medicine." That development is bringing about a long-needed rapprochement between disparate practitioners of the healing arts; general medical practitioners and psychiatrists are now talking to each other more than ever before.

Increasingly fewer physicians are looking upon psychiatrists as physicians who chose their speciality because they couldn't stand the sight of blood. Largely false, greatly overemphasized, and grossly misunderstood distinctions between mind and body, between psyche and soma, are now beginning to fade in a useful way. Let's look at some of the foregoing items more closely.

First, stress is a very popular and misunderstood term. In a recent survey of more than 3,000 people, described as representative of a cross-section of the U.S. population, fully 85 percent of the respondents felt that modern-day living involved too much stress. In another survey, the figure was 79 percent. Thus for the layman, it would seem that stress has become a generalized term, the shorthand for all undesirable pressures of modern-day living. There is too much anxiety, too much uncertainty, too many expectations, too many options. Stress is the word now most commonly used by the layman to summarize all of this. Yet it is worth looking at Selye's definition of stress: "The non-specific, that is, the common result of any demand upon the body, be it a mental or somatic demand for survival and the accomplishment of our aims." Given that definition, it is clear that we will totally avoid stress only when we have gone to our hereafter.

Stress is an integral part of everyday living. Of course those of us who may have a "heaven-or-hell" view of the hereafter, may be anticipating significantly more stress than we are experiencing right now. Selye, of course, makes a distinction between good stress and bad stress. With the term he calls "eustress," he is essentially trying to combine stress with euphoria and the feeling of well-being and exhilaration. He refers to "good" stress as eustress, and "bad" stress as distress. He then, in no way contributing to the clarity of the term, figuratively throws up his hands in surrender and says, "In ordinary conversation, I think it is perfectly acceptable to speak of stress when we mean distress, because eustress is rarely what we complain about. It simplifies matters to employ a brief terminology."

Unfortunately, it also confuses and trivializes the term stress. Nevertheless, I will defer to Dr. Selye from now on and agree that we are going to be using the word for the most part, unless otherwise stipulated, as essentially equalling distress. Many other authors have said they wished the word didn't exist.

Wouldn't it be nice to have some clear terminology. Stress, by its very nature, is an integral part of living; it is a stimulant to performance and to productivity. George Vaillant, in *Adaptation to Life*—a 40-year longitudinal study of the life-coping styles of 95 "elitist" American males — cites "anticipation" involving feelings of stress and tension as a characteristic of those who have "succeeded." Yet we have already agreed that we will use the word stress to mean distress.

In Selye's latest book, which he edited and modestly titled *Selye's Guide to Stress Research, Volume I*, he indicates that he selected eminent experts as contributors and then goes on to say, "Even among the greatest stress specialists, some fundamental problems are either ignored or misunderstood." I was really delighted to read that because at least now I won't feel bad if this presentation is rife with error. In fact, I might end up qualifying as an expert.

Unfortunately, in current stress research there are no psychobiological indicators that reliably distinguish between "good" stress and "bad" stress. Winning a million dollars in a New York State lottery and getting fired from your job are psychophysiologically identical insofar as stress and the measurable demands upon the body are concerned. Both are stressors. Both pump increased adrenalin into the system, increase the heart rate, cause the pupils to dilate, suspend normal maintenance functions, trigger out the parasympathetic system, and activate processes mediated by the sympathetic system.

In terms of current research and knowledge, we can find no reliably different results between "good" stress and "bad" stress. Yet, common sense forces me to conclude that their similarity is essentially an illusion. I would feel bad were I to get fired from a job and I would feel good if I won it big in a New York State lottery. I think I share that response with everybody in the audience. To be sure, for someone with a very weak heart, either event could precipitate a fatal heart attack. As a healthy organism, I must accept the reality that, within limits, good stressors do good things for me, my body, my sense of well-being, and bad stressors do bad things for me, my body, and my sense of well-being. That the good and bad stressors seem to have the same physiochemical effects, leads me to conclude not that they are, in fact, having the same effect on the organism, but that our knowledge is still limited and that we have much more research to do. Indeed, there is a glimmer of hope on the horizon. Within the past year or so research has been reported that seems to show consistent differences between the chemical constituents of tears caused by cinder or particles in the eye, and tears brought on by some emotion. We hope this kind of research continues, and is extended. Are tears of laughter or joy chemically the same as tears of sadness?

I said earlier that one of the results of the concept of stress is that it has led to a rapprochement among diverse healers and to a tremendous growth in behavioral medicine. That is, in my opinion, good and useful. Let me support that observation. As recently reported in *The American Psychological Association Monitor* (summer 1980), the National Cancer Institute set up a behavioral medical branch, a very unusual development in that predominantly biomedical world. They even appointed a woman psychologist as director. Other recent developments are The Behavior Medicine Society, only a few years old, and *The Journal of Behavior Medicine*. The American Psychological Association founded a new division only three years ago called the Division of Health Psychology and is planning to publish a *Journal of Health Psychology*. The previously disparate disciplines are beginning to move and work together because of a common interest in stress.

I alluded earlier to the largely false and grossly oversimplified distinction between mind and body and between psyche and soma, and I want to expand on that. It is perfectly reasonable to distinguish between mind and body, between spirit and matter, and to set up separate courses of study as though they were largely unrelated. Our natural mental predilection is to study things in chunks, in some kind of logical grouping. However, the nominalism that I referred to earlier took over in this area. Physicians treat only the body; rabbis, priests, and ministers take care of the soul. The intertwining of mind and body, flesh and spirit was surrendered to the practical need for studying things in logical coherent chunks and then to the territorial imperatives of each practitioner. The distinctions between mind and body are beginning to blur. Practitioners are beginning to treat whole people instead of aspects of people. In part, credit for this goes to pioneers in the study of stress and psychosomatic medicine — people like Cannon, Dunbar, and Selye.

It is perfectly reasonable to study the "mind" and the "body" as though they were separate from each other. I submit, however, that much more is to be gained from scholarly study of their interdependencies.

Evidence of the tremendous impact that the "mind" can have upon the "body," though "known" for a long time, is only just beginning to take hold. Consider this quote from Selye. "Most likely the *vast majority* of all maladies for which the patient seeks medical attention are predominantly due to stress, particularly psychogenic stress, which is the basis of psychosomatic medicine."

Now let me cite one piece of evidence that demonstrates how difficult it is for "long-established" and "well-known" facts to seep into the everyday awareness of the harried practitioner. In the September 1979 issue of *Across the Board,* a business publication published by the Conference Board, the cover story was on stress. The article, appropriately called "Stress," was written by Dr. Theodore Hooper, Provost for Medical Affairs and Dean of the Cornell University Medical College. In the article, he quotes Lewis Thomas who was then President of the Memorial Sloan-Kettering, as follows: "There is really no hard evidence for the effect on cancer of psychological factors, but I am fascinated with the recent work at Harvard that shows that warts are often removed by somthing like concentration. Maybe there is something to it." Now mind you, this was in 1979, and the article quotes the President of Sloan-Kettering talking about *recent work* at Harvard that shows that something like concentration may remove warts.

I then remembered reading something many years ago, and I went to an old copy of the Merck Manual, a basic medical reference for most physicians and the interns' "bible." On page 1445 of that 1961 edition, are six treatments for warts. The third one— and general practice is to put the treaments in the recommended order of trying them — is "Psychotherapy (hexing)." (The word "hexing" tells you that a psychiatrist didn't write the Merck Manual, and it tells you how psychiatry may have been looked at by "regular" medical practitioners.) Under "Psychotherapy (hexing)," the copy reads, "In young children, suggestion, accompanied by impressive but meaningless manipulation, such as painting the lesions, that is the warts, or touching them with unusual objects or exposing them to heat lamps, is often remarkably successful." So much for the "new finding" that suggestion may "cure" warts.

Today, most physicians, psychiatrists, and psychologists are willing to entertain the significant psychogenic basis for a number of illnesses and diseases — peptic ulcers, colitis, high blood pressure, migraine, asthma. However, an increasing number of diseases are being added to the roster of psychogenic etiology. One report already done and being followed-up to see if the results are replicated, is on significant differences in survival after a double mastectomy, as a function of the tendency to repress anger. Apparently, the survival time for this type of surgery is much shorter for those who, on the basis of certain tests and measurements, don't act out their rage and anger. Another recently completed study, done in this case by physicians, proposed and concluded seven guidelines, all within our control, that in their opinion could do more that all the medicine and all the physicians in the world to significantly extend the individual's life span. They are not medical guidelines and they sound very simple. At the top of the list is, don't smoke. Two, don't snack between meals. Three, drink moderately, if at all. Four, eat breakfast. Five, stay within 20 percent of the proper weight for your height and build. Six, indulge in a regular routine of exercise and seven, get eight hours of sleep.

What are some of the significant stresses of modern day living? That, of course, is a difficult question to answer. One person's stress is another's delight. The distinction between eustress and distress makes this more important. Nevertheless, if it hasn't been reported already, and it may have, there is the oft-quoted research of Holmes and Rahe who spent roughly 20 years looking into this topic. They began their study by looking at medical records and noticing the remarkable consistency of the occurrence of certain critical events in the life-history of their patients. As a result of initial interviews, study of the medical records, and finally a multi-cultural study of 5,000 respondents, they were able to rank, order, and weight the stress-impact of some 43 major life events, and by summing the weights they could make good predictions of the probability of their patients needing medical attention. What they found is that those with scores of 300 points or more had an 80 percent illness rate. Those between 150 and 300 had a 50 percent chance of being ill, and those below 150 had a 25 percent illness rate.

Holmes and Rahe found a high degree of cross-cultural consistency. In carrying out the survey, they covered Europe, Japan, the United States, and several other countries, and they found relatively little difference in the rank ordering of most events' stress impact. I want to point out some of the items on their list. For a reference point, at the top of the list, the death of your spouse was valued at 100 points.

Items directly related to work include the following: fired from the job, 45 points; retirement, 45 points; business readjustment, 39 points; change to a different line of work, 36 points; change in responsibility, 29 points; trouble with the boss, 23 points; change in work hours or conditions, 20 points; and down near the bottom, vacation, 13 points. Other items on the list could easily be directly or indirectly work-related; we have no way of knowing just from looking at the list. For example: change in financial state, 38 points; outstanding personal achievement, 28 points; change in living conditions, 25 points; change in residence, 20 points. Work-related stress is a significant part of this list. Work is one-third of our lives and it is a significant source of stresses, both positive and negative.

Another survey was done by the Atlanta Consulting Group, a mangement development firm. They surveyed 60 presidents from Fortune's top 1,000 companies. The presidents were asked to list the three most anxiety-producing situations they encounter. The list is as follows: "Failure by subordinates to accept or carry out responsibility"; 92 percent listed that. "Failure by subordinates to get critical information" was listed by 78 percent. The third item on the list was "firing someone." Bosses find that stressful in spite of their image of being hard-hearted executives; 48 percent listed that.

In 1979, The American Management Association reported another study on executive stress. They surveyed 6,000 A.M.A. members, half in top management, and half in middle management. Out of the 6,000 surveys sent, they received just over 1,400 usable replies from top management and a little over 1,200 replies from middle management. The major findings were as follows: "The results do *not* support the popular image of the harried executive for whom stress is the norm. The great majority indicated that, during the last year, stressful situations on the job arose at times, but not with great frequency." Here we can raise a methodological point. Is there or is there not a lot of executive/management stress? This study seems to say "no." But as noted, over half of the executives surveyed didn't reply. They might have been under too much stress, or too harried to answer the survey.

The most stress-producing factors on the job are work and time pressures, disparity between the manager's own goals and the expectations of the organization, and the "political" climate of the organization. Generally, those who saw the organization as a place where "who you knew" was more important than what you did, and where the rewards and growth were not predicated on performance, described the environment as "political." That environment came up as a high stressor. Off-the-job stress was reported as resulting from *ordinary* rather than acute events: financial worries, problems with children, and physical affliction. The source of stress here was not the death of someone or some critical event or accident, but rather, grinding day-to-day issues. "Grinding" or "erosive" rather than acute or dramatic also seems to describe job-related sources of stress.

What were the executives' counter-measures to stress? There were essentially three. The first one might be called "philosophical or value-prioritizing." Analyze the situation and decide what is worth worrying about and what is not. This sounds very simple, but if we could do it, it would be a good device for managing stress. It is clear that Selye, after all of his research and dedication to this area, indicates that, in his opinion, finding the proper philosophy of life gives us a way of coping with and managing stress. The second counter-measure is to delegate; if I can't get it done, I'll give it to someone else. The third one is setting action priorities. When you have got too many things going on, look at the tasks and see which are priorities.

So, to sum up, what is stress? In my opinion it refers to the human's response to situations over which he or she has lost the desired level of control. Moreover, all the measurable stress responses seem to prepare the organism for overt response — mostly "fleeing" or "fighting." This society most often demands a different response — "freezing." Stress is an unfortunate term that is widely used and widely misused. It describes a response that the organism eludes entirely only when it is dead. The term is having the fortuitous effect of bringing about better cooperation among healing practitioners. It is a term that is bringing about a better understanding of the *whole* human being and of the intimate interdependency of mind and body.

It is a term rife with stress.

REFERENCES

Benson, H. *The Relaxation Response.* Morrow, New York: 1975.

Brown, B. B. *Stress and the Art of Biofeedback.* Harper & Row, New York: 1977.

Cooper, C. L. & Marshall, J. *Understanding Executive Stress.* Petrocelli, Princeton, New Jersey: 1977.

Friedman, M. & Rosenman, R. *Type A Behavior and Your Heart.* Fawcett Book Group, New York: 1975.

Goldberg, P. *Executive Health: How to Recognize Health Danger Signals and Manage Stress Successfully.* McGraw Hill, New York: 1978.

Jackson, E. N. *Coping with the Crises in Your Life.* Hawthorne (E.T. Button), New York: 1974.

Kahn, R. L. *Organizational Stress: Studies in Role Conflict and Ambiguity.* John Wiley & Sons, New York: 1964.

Levinson, D. J., et al. *Seasons of a Man's Life.* Alfred A. Knopf, New York: 1978.

McLean, A. *Occupational Stress.* Charles C. Thomas, Springfield, Illinois: 1974.

Selye, H. *Stress Without Distress.* J. B. Lippincott, New York: 1974.

Selye, H. *The Stress of Life.* McGraw Hill, New York: 1976.

Vaillant, G. E. *Adaptation to Life.* Little-Brown, Boston: 1977.

DISCUSSION

Participants in the panel discussion, chaired by Dr. Ruocco, were: Rosemarie Carlson, Ph.D., Staff Psychologist, South Oaks Hospital; Edmund C. Neuhaus, Ph.D., Executive Director, The Rehabilitation Institute; Raul Paez, M.D., Senior Psychiatrist, South Oaks Hospital; Barton Pakull, M.D., Acting Chief, Office of Aviation Medicine, Department of Transportation, Federal Aviation Administration; and Arthur A. Stone, Ph.D., Research Scientist, Long Island Research Institute, State University of New York at Stony Brook.

Dr. Paez:

I found it very interesting that all of the speakers injected humor into their presentations. I believe that all of them were under stress and that was their way of coping. Laughter is good for people. It certainly made me relax. To have a sense of humor, to attach some sense of humor to the most difficult situations or difficult issues that anybody could confront, is helpful in coping with any type of stress. I do that quite a lot in my private practice. Some of my patients appreciate it; some of them think that I am crazy when I inject humor.

Dr. Stone:

I am going to focus on the ways people have measured life stress in the past. Holmes and Rahe, for example, have taken several events which they thought might be stressful and had people weight them, using the concept of social readjustment. Social readjustment is what everybody is talking about when they refer to change; that is, how much readjustment is needed to incorporate one of these events—marriage, divorce, a new job—into your life.

This is a very objective view of stress and I would like to contrast that with another view. Richard Lazarus approaches stress from a subjective viewpoint. He has written about psychological stress and he defines what he calls the "transactional approach" to stress; that is, what is important is not the objective stimulus out there—divorce, for instance—but how a person interprets the divorce. This leads to the rather important statement that what is stressful for some people may not be stressful for others. Furthermore, what is stressful at a particular time may not be stressful later. This is important because it means that you can't give people life-event checklists, tally up their scores, and then get an accurate view of how much stress they are under.

Holmes and Rahe's original work has been criticized lately, for another reason as well. Several studies in the last five years or so show that it is not the *amount* of change that is important but the *desirability* of the events that people are rating. One study I'm currently running examines stress in terms of the degree of control a person has over the events, how meaningful the events are to the person, the degree of change, and the degree of desirability or undesirability. It seems that change may not be as important as desirability, in respect to people's daily moods and daily somatic illnesses.

The current literature in psychology seems to be indicating that stress is indeed important, but how to *cope* with it is even more important, especially if you take the subjective approach. There have been several recent studies that discuss how different types of coping accompany different kinds of outlooks. A study by Katz in the late seventies shows that women having breast biopsies coped with the impending operation in different ways. They found, using emotional indices of coping, effectiveness of coping, and endocrine indices, that a stoic, fatalistic approach, or religious approach was much more effective than other kinds of approaches to coping. This kind of study is important because it takes into account the stimulus, the particular person, and the particular personality, when recommending how to cope with stress. I think this very individual or ideographic approach to people is important.

Dr. Pakull:

I worked as a psychiatrist for the Peace Corps before coming to the Federal Aviation Administration 10 years ago. Prior to that I was a military psychiatrist in Vietnam, working especially with pilots under combat conditions. From all of my experiences with military and civilian pilots—working in the field of alcoholism rehabilitation, working with air traffic controllers, working with Peace Corps volunteers, and working with people in a combat situation—I am at variance with most of the other speakers. I think that the word "stress" is a useless term, and that its use creates problems and doesn't promote greater understanding. I think we would do well to have this conference without *ever* using the word "stress."

I would generally define the stress hypothesis, as it is used currently, as the proposition that adult life events or situations can cause significant changes in personality or have significant or longlasting effects on mental health.

I don't believe that the stress hypothesis works, that it is true or that it is even useful. In fact, it has potential dangers and brings us more difficulties than gains both in understanding behavior and in the area of political and social change. I even question the psychosomatic hypothesis; especially the corollary that dysfunction in certain end organs implies an emotional precursor.

I believe that *"stress relief programs"* have become a social science cottage industry, organized by people who have something to gain from the concept of "stress," in order to push their solutions. For instance, I have seen stress-relief programs or philosophies or teachings used to promote the use of minor tranquilizers. I happen to agree with a growing number of physicians that the overuse of minor tranquilizers is a considerable public health problem. I take issue with and deeply resent physicians who use stress to promote the use of minor tranquilizers.

I will give one last example. I have a great deal of interest and experience in the field of alcohol rehabilitation. I belong to that segment in the alcohol rehabilitation field that believes, for tactical as well as for theoretical reasons, that stress has nothing to do with the development of alcoholism, and as a concept it offers no aid in the rehabilitation of alcoholics.

Whenever you use stress or imply that alcohol is a coping mechanism, you are undermining the alcoholic rehabilitation effort. People experience a great many problems when they are alcoholics. When they are rehabilitated they are the same people, but they have fewer difficulties because they don't drink. They still have some of the difficulties they had when they were drinking, *but they don't drink.* A practicing alcoholic would like you to believe that he drinks because of stress, to get you off his back so he can keep drinking. He uses the issue of stress or external influence as a maneuver, as part of the denial system. If you buy into "stress" when you are dealing with alcoholics, you are not going to rehabilitate them.

Dr. Carlson:

Stress can be viewed as a composite, consisting of a stressor, the vulnerability or the particular reaction of the individual, and the supportive context. There is an agent, a host, and the environment.

My focus will be upon the host or the individual. By the time a person comes to my office, something in the system has failed. Something has broken down. He feels overwhelmed. He is unable to cope with a stressor, whether it is real or imagined. I believe that stress usually involves a loss of some kind; either a real loss, an imagined one, or an anticipated one. If the supportive network of the individual fails to offer adequate relief, he or she may turn to a professional as the last resort. He may have attempted various coping mechanisms, some of which can be considered healthy, and some of which are so maladaptive that they create more misery than they are designed to alleviate. Usually these are aimed at removing the tension as quickly as possible, rather than really taking a look at the problem and trying to figure out a solution.

Many adolescents, for example, attempt to cope with stress by self-medicating with alcohol or drugs, and that leads to a whole series of other problems for them. Some people blame others for their problems; they see themselves as victims and feel justified in retaliating and lashing out in a hostile way. My task in treatment is to reduce the vulnerability of the individual. Some of the techniques that I have had success with are relaxation therapy, biofeedback, hypnotherapy, systematic desensitization, and psychotherapy.

We try to give the individual in treatment a sense of hope, a sense of confidence that he will be able to understand the problem. We give him a handle on the problem, a way of looking at it and dealing with it so that it makes sense to him. As he learns, for example, to control his blood pressure through the use of biofeedback, his success in this area then generalizes to to other areas in his life. His confidence that he will be able to manage his difficulties then spreads.

As for healthy ways of coping with stress, different ideas are offered—one is to help the individual identify the problem and break it down into manageable pieces so that he can realistically work on one thing at a time. It is important that he turn to other people and try to get help from them rather than isolate himself and become even more depressed and alienated.

Another important thing is to help the person separate reality factors from non-reality factors. When a person becomes anxious he starts to experience all kinds of irrational thoughts—something is wrong with me; I am going to have a heart attack, I am going to faint, I am going crazy. These thoughts increase the anxiety, with the result that the physiological symptoms of anxiety get exacerbated, causing thoughts to become even more irrational. As the disordered thinking escalates, the anxiety increases until a situation of spiraling panic occurs. It is necessary to step in and help the victim of this process to break this cycle by learning not to panic in response to symptoms of anxiety, and by pointing out reality so he can learn to differentiate between rational and irrational ideas.

Dr. Neuhaus:

Just as everyone's viewpoint is highly idiosyncratic and reflects their own ideas about their professional life, so will mine. With all due respect to our Federal Aviation Administration psychiatrist, I think he flies in the face of what we all know exists in the world, namely dis-ease. We all have periods of dis-ease—distress, stress, anxiety, uncomfortable situations. As a psychoanalyst, working with people for over a quarter of a century, trying to understand myself and knowing I become more ignorant every year and that makes me wiser, I have come to feel very strongly that *how* we face stress or dis-ease or discomfort, reflects the kind of person we are, the way we look at life, people, and things around us. Unfortunately, as human beings we can only communicate orally or with the written word. One of the best ways that all of us can face this dis-ease is to realize that life is unfair and to keep in mind the epigram, "Living well is the best revenge."

One of my great models was Gordon Allport, who talked about the mature individual. I would like to adapt what he said. Achieving maturity is to develop a philosophy of life, to have for yourself some meaning of what this mortal coil is all about. Whether your philosophy is religion, intellect, mathematics, or science is irrelevant. But we all should develop some framework that enables us to interpret what the world means to us.

Secondly, I think to be mature is to be able to have a sense of humor. A sense of humor implies something very important. Not the sense of humor we saw here in many instances, which was forced, constrained, or full of anxiety, but the sense of humor that says, hey, I am a human being which means I am fallible. I'm screwed up in a lot of ways and I have a lot of problems, but I can look at myself and laugh.

Lastly, to periodically be able to be mature, to reevaluate where I am going, what I am doing, to really look at myself objectively.

I am very impressed with the primacy or the effectiveness of the human mind. I have seen people in combat survive mortal wounds because of their will to live. Norman Cousins, in his *Anatomy of an Illness*, tells how a self-prescribed dose of laughter helped him overcome a mortal disease. He is now teaching at Stanford Medical School, making physicians aware of the importance of the mind in healing. René Dubos, the Nobel Prize-winning biologist, calls himself a despairing optimist. He despairs because the world is a pretty bad place and there are numerous catastrophies or stresses, but is an optimist because when he looks back upon mankind's achievements, and achievements to come, he sees that the bombed-out cities have new opera houses today, the defeated nations are in the forefront of economic progress. We *do* rise from the ashes.

My plea, as a clinical psychologist who works with disturbed people and in the community where people come from the hospitals, is to realize the importance of positive outlook that has meaning for you, and that enables you to be self-critical and laugh at yourself and man's condition.

Dr. Ruocco:

I think the panel represent a tremendous range of very interesting viewpoints. I really don't think they are as diverse as they sound. Maybe some would like to polarize more than others. I am not sure of that. In any case, I think I ought to change my title from moderator to referee.

Audience:

I am an occupational health nurse. Would you say that stress is a misnomer? Should it be called anxiety?

Dr. Ruocco:

I think anxiety is a *kind* of stress. It is *one* kind of stress among many others.

Dr. Stone:

I tend to disagree. I go along with the idea that stress is a set of cognitions prompted by environmental stimuli and possibly leading to anxiety or physical disability, or nothing for that matter. I wouldn't view anxiety as a stress, but rather as an outcome.

Dr. Ruocco:

I agree with Dr. Pakull that the term is an abomination. I have problems with the term. If we want to use the word stress in its most general, technical sense, it is not only OK to have stress, it is good, necessary, and inevitable if you are going to be alive. I mean that literally. What we have been talking about, however, is *distress* or *dis-ease*. I think that is a much better term. We must distinquish between negative stress and positive stress. In that sense, anxiety is a particular kind of negative stress, distress, or dis-ease. Certainly the literature uses stress and distress interchangeably. There is no question about that. So it is a confused area from the semantic standpoint.

Dr. Neuhaus:

This conference is about stress. I equate it with dis-ease, and that's the term that seems most important to me.

Audience:

Would you say that stress is the cause of anxiety?

Dr. Neuhaus:

No, I wouldn't. I would subsume everything we are talking under stress.

Dr. Stone:

In literature there have been three or four different definitions of stress. In *The Journal of Human Stress*, Hans Selye wrote an article called, "Confusion and Controversy in the Stress Field." The theme was confusion over what stress is and isn't, and it is the confusion that exists here. It was defined several ways. One, stress is a stimulus; two, stress is an outcome; and three, stress is an interaction between both stimulus and outcome. We must arrive at our definitions here, or else we are going to get all confused about what stress produces, versus what it is.

Dr. Neuhaus:

I would like to ask the audience, what do you think stress is? Tell me some of the stresses that you have experienced.

Audience:

To solve the problem, we have to define what the problem is. Industry says it is occupational and safety hazards, heat, lighting, dust. It is also marital problems, divorce. I think that we ought to do away with the term stress. It is too general.

Dr. Pakull:

The stress hypothesis, as it has been presented here, has ranged from the unsupportable to the trivial. Things have been said about the relationship between stress and illness that are scientifically unsupportable. Also, to say there are good stresses, bad stresses, distresses, and so on, is trivial. What I object to is when we start using that word to promote our own little empires, such as the so-called stress relief programs. When we use stress in this way, I begin to object to it; not only because its meaning is inane, but also because it is used to rationalize almost any kind of behavioral or social program.

Audience:

I am a clinical psychologist. Why aren't we talking about productivity? We are talking only of stress as a way of avoiding the issue of why we are not producing or how we *should be* pro-

ducing. Stress is being used as an excuse for poor productivity.
I agree with Dr. Pakull that often mental health programs tri-
vialize every issue into something that is a psychiatric or psychological problem.

It seems that if we substituted loss of self-esteem or loss of
a support sytem, it would cover at least 90 percent of life change
units such as divorce, separation, jail sentences, physical illness,
etc. I would like to promote speaking more about loss—whether
actual or threatened—and relate that to how we produce or don't
produce.

Dr. Pakull:

Of course what you say is true. But it is too simple, too obvious to capture public attention. Further, there is sometimes a
social need to make an illness or disease out of certain social
injustices or social problems. This is the way to get attention.
You get funding by talking about something in medical terms.
We tend to stray into the medical field in our use of words in
order—in a misplaced humanistic way—to get attention for things
we want to promote, or injustices we want to correct. This is a
very poor social policy and bad science.

That is also part of my objection to the use of the word
stress and the way it is now being promoted in the United States.
We don't need to hide injustice behind the label of disease. Injustice stands for itself. Social issues don't need medical ration-
alizations. We don't have to justify social or political redress by
saying this or that injustice causes illness.

Dr. Ruocco:

The old model of alcoholism was that it was a lack of will-
power, a lack of character. Obviously, within the last 10 to 15
years it has gained acceptance as a disease. Do you accept that?

Dr. Pakull:

No, I disagree with both views.

Dr. Ruocco:

We have to admire your consistency.

Dr. Pakull:

There is a tendency to think of alcoholism in terms of a moral failing and a lack of will, and we know that is not so. It is a condition characterized by a loss of control over the use of alcohol, with the emergence of deleterious consequences in the areas of health, or social or personal functioning. Most people prefer to call it a disease in order to bring it away from the stage we were at 20 years ago when it was considered a moral failure. To legitimatize the "treatment" of alcoholics, we called it a disease. To relieve the stigma of alcoholism, we call it a disease. You could consider alcoholism as a condition, a phenomenon, a category, and a label. Certainly it has medical consequences. Although you can consider it a disease, I have reservations about this approach.

My first reservation relates to the connotation that a disease is beyond your control. That is, the disease happens to you and you are not responsible for what occurs. The issue of responsibility is very crucial to alcoholism rehabilitation on an individual level. That issue has been faced this way: You are *not* responsible for being an alcoholic, but you *are* responsible for doing something about it. One reason for objecting to the disease concept is because, theoretically, it clouds the issue of responsibility.

Dr. Ruocco:

It is now defined as a disease by all the "authorities" (whatever that means): the armed forces, the American Psychiatric Association, the American Medical Association. That is irrelevant to you?

Dr. Pakull:

No, it is not irrelevant, it just tells us that different agencies want to bring this condition under their aegis and control. That is my second objection to simply calling alcoholism a disease. It implies that alcoholism is only to be managed, as a social phenomenon and condition, by physicians or by psychiatrists. In fact, I believe that this condition is mostly best handled by the afflicted people through self-help groups, sometimes with the help of physicians and other professionals. These are my main concerns with the disease concept.

Audience:

I'm with the New York State Department of Labor. I'm kicking around the concepts because I, too, am looking for a handle. In the physical sense, stress is applying pressure to an object: a piece of metal, or structure. Applying external forces. To bring that a step further to the process affecting the human condition; stress results from the denial of predictable and anticipated experiential factors in the human condition.

Dr. Stone:

Selye first used the term stress to define its psychobiological aspect. Certainly the term stress had been used in engineering way before that. I have been a stress researcher for the last two years, and in the studies that I do with community members, I never use the word stress. Maybe that tells you something about it. What I do is ask them, on a daily basis, to look at what they did today, and rate how they felt about certain dimensions that I've already mentioned here. Then I watch and I see what happens to the people thereafter.

Dr. Neuhaus:

But you still define it operationally, don't you?

Dr. Stone:

Let me tell you how I defined it originally in the studies that generated the event list. I asked people to jot down things in their environment which were significant to them or were emotionally arousing for them. I don't know what stress is because I don't know which one of those dimensions, or which kind of daily events produce later dysfunction or later mood changes, for example. My point was that you don't have to use the word stress. You can say, look, I am going to be an empiricist about this and I am going to try to look for connections in a fairly scientific and rigorous way; these things seem to be important for those people, let's try to go in and help them if they need help.

Dr. Neuhaus:

A patient came to me last week, a 58-year-old woman, a health professional. For several years she had had family-related problems; now she was having a work problem. She is a caring woman who is a troubleshooter in a hospital, trying to be an ombudsman. She created new systems, seeing that people got the proper follow-up, stepping on a lot of political toes. For 10 years she survived doing this kind of work, but she told me she was thinking about retiring.

She told me that the medical director who was her support all these years had left and the toes that she had been stepping on over the years suddenly got strong and told her she was next on the blacklist. And, little by little, she was losing recognition for what she was doing. She was feeling increasingly powerless. She was feeling increasingly frustrated in not being able to any longer do the really good things, because of the empire builders and the political system. She is in crisis. She is experiencing an enormous amount of stress, a lot of dissatisfactions. What was very important was that she was experiencing a loss, a very important loss, a loss of being accepted, a loss of status. And it was way beyond her control.

This was, as a consequence, beginning to affect her productivity. She was no longer as energetic, no longer doing the many things that she used to do, and was now talking about retirement.

Allied to that is my experience as a director of an agency. I have 80 people working for me, primarily mental health professionals. And, as I jokingly say, I have 80 different problems—more problems than the 400 clients we serve. In a work situation it is very important for another human being to know that the employer is, more or less, a good and caring "parent." The ability to show people that you hold them in esteem, that you care about them, that you accept them, has a lot to do with stress and productivity.

Audience:

I am a consultant to industry. Part of my job is helping people *create* the stress necessary to cause productivity. We call it incentive programs. All I hear about is absenteeism, illness, accidents; nothing relating to an industrial application of productivity. I have heard very little about the positive tensions and the motivations that are also part of stress. I think that these are essential elements to a productive society. If we don't talk about how to corral them and use them and direct them, I think we are just spinning our wheels.

Dr. Ruocco:

With too little stress, you have boredom, indifference, total lack of productivity. But go *over* the "right" amount of stress, and you decrease productivity. The point made by the panel is how do you measure stress? What might be a tiny bit of stress to me may be unbearable stress to you.

How do you apply that to your company, your employees? How do you measure it? I think we can get some consensus on a healthy working environment. Certainly, that environment would be wholesome, giving, caring, concerned. I think the consensus would say those are relevant to productivity. But I think we would also find that productivity increases with a fair performance review by management. That would be very high on the list of attributes for a productive working environment. Not knowing where one stands is regarded as a highly stressful situation. I can assure you, having had wide experience with that, that it is very difficult to get management to give an honest performance feedback. Management works with two sets of books. They can tell an employee he is doing just fine, and the minute the employee steps out the door, they will call personnel and demand that that employee be fired.

One of the toughest things to do is to talk objectively and maturely to your employee about what it is you want him or her to continue doing, and what it is you want him or her to change. Management feels the stress of treating an employee as a human being. They refuse to do it, so they set up conditions, circumstances, subcultures within the working organization that everyone finds uncomfortable. That is the tie-in between stress and productivity: feelings of discomfort, feelings of ambiguity. We don't need surveys to tell us that no matter how tough-minded a manager appears in certain situations, it is very difficult for him or her to fire someone. They feel uncomfortable. They feel negative stress.

So, you have employee discomfort and you have management discomfort. It is reasonable to infer that when these feelings come up in a work environment, there is a problem that can be addressed in very direct, very simple terms. You don't need psychologists, you don't need physicians, nurses, anyone. You just need a performance review program. You need managers trained to talk to others about performance in a constructive way.

Dr. Neuhaus:

What you are really encouraging is talking to employees and being open and honest and respectful.

Dr. Ruocco:

Right. Accept a person as a human being; attack his or her performance, if necessary, but not the person. Say, "Look, Phil, Mary, these are several of the things that you have been doing that are super, but there are some other areas where I have some problems." Then ask what you, as the manager, are doing to cause it? A lot of managers won't even go that far because they think it may be a surrender of the boss-subordinate relationship: their status. You can educate them to do that. One of the most mature things one can do is constructive sharing of work experiences and you, as the boss, should be doing that. We are past the stages of whips; we are at the state in management and at a level of sophistication that requires us to treat others as human beings. We must respect their needs for information, their needs for growth, and tell them honestly when they are doing well and doing poorly. Respectfully.

Dr. Paez:

As for a practical answer to productivity, it is interesting to read how Japan is coping with communal problems in their companies. Some factories have punching bags where employees can take out their resentment at the company. Many Japanese employees are exercising before they get to work. They jog together. Whatever they do, they do something physical together. I don't see why this cannot be tried here on a smaller scale, to see if it would work with us, too. Sometimes we look for very complicated answers to simple questions.

I asked a Swedish professor of psychiatry how they cope with stress and productivity. He gave me a classic example—the Saab factory. Some union leaders visited the factory and upon entering the grounds they thought they were in a public park. They saw greenery and flowers and shrubs. It was the entrance to the truck division of the factory. When they went into the factory, it was extremely comfortable. They found that on coffee-breaks the workers could ride their bicycles, read a book, or play tennis. So many of our situations are just the opposite of that. I have to eat lunch in 10 minutes. I have no choice; I must eat in 10 minutes because I have to meet a deadline.

Dr. Carlson:

I would like to speak about the special stress facing women in work situations. Many of my patients are professional women who have various kinds of work inhibitions. They feel that they want to produce, they want to do well, but something is stopping them. The basis of the conflict is usually the fear of some kind of loss. It is traumatic for a woman to take a course in life that departs radically from her mother's course. She feels that her mother will disapprove, her mother will be envious, jealous, angry. She has to struggle with feelings of losing a certain amount of femininity. She is concerned about losing involvement with her husband, family life, children. Today is my son's birthday and I wonder, should I be at home baking a cake?

Solutions for industry are really not my forté, but a couple of ideas come to mind. One is to arrange a situation which would facilitate the open exchange of ideas and feelings among women, giving them a chance to meet with one another, perhaps in assertiveness training or various other training courses that could be provided by companies. The women would see that there isn't something wrong with struggling with these kinds of feelings. Maybe women in the work force need more support than men do. I believe many women think that they are doing something wrong by working outside the home and that they really should be at home taking care of babies, cooking, and so forth. The problem of women are special and need to be treated in a special way.

Dr. Ruocco:
   I agree that there are special concerns in view of the increasing numbers of women in business. Most companies are creating programs to address these special problems.

Audience:
   Neither in the classical nor in the religious literature of the Hebrews and Greeks, do I find anyting we can translate into the word "stress." Literally. There are many, many passages in the Old Testament and in the New Testament and in classical Greek writings that talk of distress. Distress is defined as when the individual can no longer function or produce in a manner that is acceptable to others as well as to himself or herself. It is a reduction of the power or the energy to function in a manner rewarding to self and others. In a sense, we could say that the opposite of that would be stress. In ancient literature, when we talk about being distressed, it means being incapacitated in some way. But stress was not in the ancient literature. We use this as a modern English word, so in a sense, thinking philosophically, it is a very *positive* word.
   This conference seems to emphasize that the human being is a product of the environment or of systems or of organizations, and that the individual cannot do much about distress or malfunctioning or unhappiness. By the way, in ancient literature, the unhappy individual was the one who was in distress. The happy individual was the one who was inspired and very functional in all dimensions, to self, to God, and to others. Happiness and productivity are not dependent upon the circumstances you find yourself in, or the people you are surrounded by, but upon

what is happening from within; in other words, by what your philosophy is, what your views are, or what you think life is all about.

Dr. Neuhaus:

The free individual, the person who can function to the optimum level, is the one who takes full responsibility for what he is experienceing or going through at the moment. You can cope with the slings and arrows because there is something within you, saying, "I am secure. I have developed my meaning and my sense of purpose and I will hold fast to that until the end."

After World War II, I was in counter-intelligence and did a lot of investigation work with concentration camp victims. The one thing concentration camp victims had was their identities. As people walked into the gas chambers, they would mutter and mumble their names. That was their sense of identity and maybe that is the answer to what you said. One thing we all have is our own identity, and the degree to which we feel strong or weak about it reflects how we operate in the world.

Audience:

The issue of the term stress has been bothering me. I have been unable to figure out if stress is a cause, or a result, or both. Dr. Pakull's statement that it is a condition rings true to me. Stress is a condition of needs disparity, whether physical or emotional, whether within you or by expectation of someone else.

On the Holmes Rahe scale, the loss of a spouse is rated as 100—very stressful. But what about the person who wants nothing more in life than to lose that spouse?

Dr. Ruocco:

I agree with you. We all see the problems in that. On that scale, death of a loved one and going to jail are rated very near marriage. I am serious. It makes the list look a little bit foolish. The other point made is the idiosyncratic nature of stress. We play poker. I win, you lose, OK? Same stress. It is a matter of measuring.

Dr. Stone:

Social readjustment is what everyone is equating with stress. They use it interchangeably. What I did in one study was to ask people to give me ratings on social readjustment for 43 events, just like Holmes and Rahe did. I duplicated the ratings in part of the study. In part two, I asked them to rate the stress of each one of these events. In that study, the ratings don't line up one to one. Not at all.

Audience:

What are some stressful situations or environments that increase productivity? I have a whole list of things that decrease stress and would make the work environment less stressful, but there is a point of diminishing return. What are some suggestions for constructive stress that can be developed in industry?

Dr. Paez:

It is very important to take into account the things that we bring into work, such as problems from home, which a supervisor or manager has very little to do with. So, we bring stress to work and productivity *suffers*. Then, we know that the stress that originates at work could be positive or negative. One of the things that comes to mind is incentives. It is very bad if you work in a situation where there is no incentive and no rewards. I have a patient who says she can't do her work because the 10 people under her come to her with their personal problems. They bring their problems to work. So, because she wants to increase production, she listens to everybody and you know what happens? Nothing is accomplished. She doesn't solve a single problem for a single person. It is total chaos.

It is extremely important for management to understand that some problems at work originate outside. In other words, study what you are getting into. It is very important to take into consideration some of the stressors that we bring to work, and put them into the frame of reference of how productive you can be. If you have a headache and you don't have aspirin, and you know that aspirin is going to relieve your headache, how good is your production going to be unless you get those two aspirin?

Audience:

Can stress be a cover-up for other types of feelings? The woman mentioned who was a hospital administrator had a feeling of stress. It is obvious that stress was a cover-up for anxiety, for loss of self-esteem.

Dr. Pakull:

I think you very clearly made the point that I am trying to make. You have to look behind what a person is saying and find out the specific problem. Is it a mental health professional problem? It may not be. But you are certainly obligated to treat the problem as it is and not make it into something else. Of course people disguise the kind of problem they have when they come to see a professional. Part of the skill of the professional is to decode the problem. For instance, someone comes in and says, "I'm under stress at my job." It turns out that, no, his "stress" is not at his job.

Dr. Neuhaus:

Dr. Pakull, you who disavowed the concept of stress, resorted to it. Why?

Dr. Pakull:

To finish, this man is unhappy or he is under pressure, but the difficulty may not be the work. Perhaps, it is because he is married to one person but is having an affair with another, and this personal problem affects his work.

Dr. Neuhaus:

It's still a difficulty. It's still a negative reaction.

Dr. Ruocco:

I think there is agreement on that. The issue we have returned to is the word. I think there is a consensus that it causes a problem, but there *is* a reality out there. To loosely quote Selye, I say let's be sloppy and use the word. I think we all agree that short of ridding the English language of the word, we must make it less trivial, less of a dumping ground, more precise.

Chapter 6

MEDICAL MANAGEMENT OF STRESS

Stephen D. Shappell, M.D.*

* Dr. Stephen D. Shappell has had a long term interest in emotional stress and its role in cardiovascular disease. He received his A.B. from Columbia University in 1961 and his M.D. from Cornell University Medical College in 1965. Medical internship, two years of medical residency, and two years of cardiology fellowship were served at the University of Washington, in Seattle. He was a Major in the U.S. Air Force, stationed as a cardiologist at Wilford Hall U.S.A.F. Hospital in San Antonio, Texas. During his various faculty positions, including the University of Texas Medical School in San Antonio, University of Oklahoma College of Medicine, and currently as Clinical Associate Professor of Medicine at Cornell University Medical College, he has published material on the role of variant angina and the induction of cardiovascular arrhythmia with REM Sleep. Dr. Shappell is a former teaching scholar of the American Heart Association and is a Fellow of the American College of Physicians, American College of Cardiology, American Heart Association Council of Clinical Cardiology, American College of Chest Physicians, New York Cardiological Society, and American College of Angiology. He is a member of the Suffolk Heart Group with offices in Bay Shore and Smithtown, New York.

Before we consider the medical management of stress, let us first examine what we know of the role of stress in the production of systemic disease. In regard to viral illness, for example, there is increasing evidence that prolonged emotional stress makes one more susceptible to the development of disease from exposure to a variety of viruses. Additionally, similar studies have suggested that prolonged emotional stress induces greater susceptibility to certain bacterial illnesses.

On occasion, among military recruits at boot camp, the meningococcus has appeared to colonize the pharynx of recruits as well as the officer corps. Systemic illness, however—fever, sepsis, shock—has been predominantly limited to the boot camp recruit, who has marched hard, has been under significant emotional stress, is in a new environment, and sleeps relatively little. Whether emotional stress diminishes polymorphonuclear leukocyte function in counteracting bacterial infection, alters lymphocyte function in the setting of viral illness, or has a general depressive effect on immune function, is not clear. We are all familiar with the apparent role of emotional stress and acid production with ulcer disease. Veterinarians studying duodenal ulcer, often use pigs as their model. Pigs, tightly packed in a pen where it is a struggle for food and water and where there is no freedom of movement, exhibit a significant ulcer incidence within two months.

It is in the realm of cardiovascular disease in general, and sudden cardiac death more specifically, however, that the role of stress appears to have its most potent effect. Since, of the more than 700,000 individuals who die each year of heart disease in the United States, 450,000 die sudden cardiac death, the magnitude of the problem becomes clear.

Let us focus, then, on sudden cardiac death since it is the greatest cause of death in the group of adults under the age of 65. Of all people who die annually of heart disease, sudden cardiac death is the *initial manifestation of heart disease* in full a 25 percent of this group. Sudden unexpected (natural) death is defined as death occurring instantaneously or within 24 hours of the onset of acute symptoms or signs (American Heart Association definition). Let us examine the characteristics of sudden unexpected cardiac death, define *the role of stress* in the precipitation of sudden death, and then address the *medical management of stress in an effort to prevent sudden death.* I will not focus here on the use of psychotropic drugs. Their use can be amply covered by the psychiatrists at this conference.

Seventy percent of patients with sudden death had been under the care of a physician for coronary heart disease, diabetes, or hypertension. Twenty percent significantly delayed seeking medical care after the onset of symptoms. Thirty percent had seen a physician within one month of death. Of sudden death victims, 92 percent die with ventricular fibrillation, 8 percent with asystole. Seventy-five percent of sudden cardiac deaths occur at home, 4 percent at work, 8 percent in the ambulance, and 8 percent in the emergency room (Simon et al, 1973).

Approximately 3 percent of sudden deaths are associated with vigorous physical exertion. Sixty-five percent had prodromal symptoms. *Unusual fatigue* was the major premonitory symptom. Dyspnea, chest pain, and emotional changes were less frequent. Because fatigue is such a common complaint in the physician's office, it is often difficult to discern amongst the many patients with this complaint, the ones at risk for subsequent sudden death. The majority of sudden death victims have significant coronary disease. Other causes of sudden death include prolonged QT interval syndrome, cardiomyopathies, aortic stenosis, degenerative heart disease, mitral valve prolapse syndrome, and pulmonary embolism. In such studies as the Medic I from Seattle, (Cobb et al, 1975) 80 percent of patients resuscitated from out of hospital ventricular fibrillation had not, after CCU assessment, suffered an acute myocardial infarction. Thus, the sudden ventricular fibrillation was an "electrical accident."

In this group of patients, that is, those patients who have suffered ventricular fibrillation, have been resuscitated, and who have not evolved an acute myocardial infarction, there is a significant increase in sudden cardiac death within two years of follow-up compared with those who had ventricular fibrillation, and had suffered a myocardial infarction (Schaffer et al, 1975; & Baum et al, 1974). Thus, ventricular fibrillation, resuscitation, and no infarction means that that area of the heart muscle is a "sitting time bomb." Later in this discussion, we will try to elaborate on the thesis that, for a *given magnitude* of coronary disease and left ventricular dysfunction, it is the brain, via emotional stress-related mechanisms, that determines the time of sudden death. In patients with, for example, three-vessel coronary disease and poor ventricular function, the death rate with optimal medical therapy may be 15 percent per year. The individual's response to emotional stress appears to differentiate those who die in year one, versus those who are still alive at year four.

Whereas the presence of left ventricular hypertrophy, hypertension, and chronic smoking are the three major risk factors, in addition to the presence of coronary heart disease, diabetes, and elevated cholesterol in patients at risk for sudden death, 13 percent of patients dying sudden death have no significant obstructive coronary disease (Kuller et al, 1966).

Rahe and colleagues (Rahe et al, 1973 & 1974), realizing the emotional role of death of a spouse, divorce, and loss of a job in the psychophysiologic induction of sudden death, used a survey of life change units (LCU) in the study of patients who died sudden death versus a control group. They used a questionnaire assessing these life change units. An LCU relative weight represents the degree of life change and readjustment necessary for an individual to cope with each life event. The events covered included separation from wife due to marital problems, separation from wife due to her going to work, recent marriage, addition of a new family member in the home, recent illness, change in sleeping habits, unpaid bills leading to threatened legal action, high debt, change in religious or political activities, death of a spouse, divorce, sexual difficulties, major decisions regarding a son or daughter leaving home. Individuals who died sudden death had significantly increased their LCU total within the six months prior to sudden death.

Myers and Dewar (1975) found that acute psychological stress was the most significant precipitant of sudden death in the group they studied. Engel (1971, 1976 & 1978) has emphasized psychological factors in precipitating sudden death. The 170 patients he described had experienced the following life settings: (1) death of a person close to them; (2) acute grief; (3)

threat of losing a person close to them; (4) mourning of a person's death, or an anniversary of the death; (5) loss of self-esteem; (6) threat of personal injury; (7) sudden release from danger; (8) sudden elation, extreme joy—particularly after prolonged stress.

Patients dying sudden death or experiencing intense emotion often give up, feeling uniformly trapped or cornered by circumstances beyond their control. In studies of voodoo culture, it appears that if you were hexed to die and you believed in the hex, you die sudden death. If you felt it was inevitable, you "gave up" and died (Cannon, 1957).

Lown and colleagues (1978) have demonstrated that psychologic stress induced in animals makes them more susceptible to ventricular fibrillation.

The debate regarding the mechanism of sudden death focuses upon those researchers who emphasize the sympathetic nervous system in precipitation of ventricular fibrillation versus those who emphasize the parasympathetic nervous system—with vagally mediated bradycardia, asystole and ventricular fibrillation (VF) secondary to bradycardia. The problem is complex.

The heart's rate is presumably controlled by the balance of sympathetic nervous system (beta stimulation) and parasympathetic nervous system (vagal mediation) on the sinus node. If one gives a patient a full blocking dose of I.V. Propranolol (i.e. maximal beta blockade) and a fully blocking dose of I.V. Atropine (i.e. maximal beta blockade), this patient is now said to have a double blockade, and is theoretically denervated. Such a patient, however, placed on a treadmill, exhibits a normal increase in heart rate—suggesting the existence of other neurotransmitters, yet to be defined. Indeed, there are now many neurotransmitters that have been defined; some of them will no doubt be discovered to have a role in psychophysiologic changes that lead to sudden death.

In studies of a parachutist who was monitored during a jump, his heart rate was 190 beats per minute during the jump itself. As soon as he landed he fractured his ankle. The sudden pain from the ankle fracture was associated with an almost instantaneous drop of the sinus tachycardia from 190 beats per minute to a vagal mediated 40 beats per minute. This was accomplished in approximately two seconds. It is the apparent disproportion of sympathetic and parasympathetic influences on the cardiovascular system that leads to neural confusion and sudden death.

In classic studies regarding the role of stress and sudden death, Dr. Robert Eliot of the University of Nebraska (1974 & 1977) studied the personnel at The Kennedy Space Center during the big push of the Moon Program in the late sixties and early seventies. The evidence of stress included inordinately high incidences of alcoholism, divorce, and drug abuse. Annual sudden death rates were far in excess of the usual percentages seen in other male populations in Florida. Although the traditional risk factors such as smoking and elevated cholesterol were no greater, psychoneuroticism appeared to be the major independent contributor to sudden death.

Emotional stress has been demonstrated to precipitate coronary artery spasm. REM-sleep-induced coronary artery spasm, often found in variant angina, is an early morning phenomenon. Central vagal mediation appears to precipitate coronary spasm.

In patients with mitral valve prolapse and life threatening arrhythmias, there appears to be an inordinate number of abnormalities on the Minnesota Multiphasic Personality Inventory (MMPI) scales compared with mitral valve prolapse patients who have no life-threatening arrhythmias (Shappell et al, 1974).

How can we be more certain, however, that sudden death did have a psychologic basis?

Dr. Eliot has demonstrated a characteristic pathologic lesion referred to as *coagulative myocytolysis*, seen in patients dying sudden cardiac death (1974 & 1977). This lesion, which can be produced in animals by infusion of a high dose of cathecholamines (1978), is seen in patients dying with head injury and pheochromocytoma. It is a characteristic lesion in victims who die sudden death *after* a mugging and who had little or no physical trauma. It is also found in monitored test pilots who have lost control of their test plane and have died sudden death before the airplane actually crashed(Buell & Eliot, in press).

Additionally, patients at risk for sudden cardiac death with atherosclerotic heart disease, demonstrate altered platelet function. Epinephrine infusion in animals, and electrical pacing induced angina in man appear to alter platelet function. Since coronary spasm appears to be partly related to platelet released thromboxane A_2, and since emotional stress appears to enhance platelet deposition and aggregation in coronary arteries, this may be one of many pathophysiologic links to psychologic stress and sudden death. Since alpha blockers can block reflux coronary vasoconstriction elicited by the cold pressor test, this is another direct link of a neurogenic mechanism in the pathophysiology of sudden death.

How, then, can stress be managed so as to prevent sudden death in the susceptible population—particularly those with coronary heart disease, whether or not the presence of coronary disease is known to them.

The Relaxation Response, popularized by Dr. Herbert Benson, (1977) is the basis for some of the changes seen in transcendental meditation. Frequency of premature ventricular contractions(PVCs) can be diminished, and blood pressure can be mildly controlled with these techniques. Whether the regular use of the relaxation response prevents sudden death is certainly not established at this time, despite the greater state of serenity it provides.

Hypnosis has not been demonstrated to be effective in long-term behavior modification and, at this time, is not likely to help prevent sudden death. In regard to the role of coronary spasm induced sudden death, the use of centrally mediated and peripheral alpha blockers, and direct coronary vasodilators such as the slow calcium channel blockers (Nifedipine)® appears to be promising, but requires further study. To be sure, these drugs do not prevent or manage stress, but they alter the neurophysiologic consequences of stress.

Standard anti-anxiety drugs appear to decrease the frequency of PVCs in a coronary care setting, but have not been shown to have a clear benefit in prevention of sudden death. Phenothiazine derivatives and tricylic anti-depressants, in the presence of heart disease, alter the ST-T waves and QT interval. Their general arrhythmic potential often counterbalances their central nervous system anti-depressant effects in the cardiac patient and may have a net negative result.

The use of beta blockers appears to be efficacious in preventing sudden death, particularly in patients with coronary disease and past anterior wall infarct (Ahlmark et al, 1974; Multicenter International Study, 1975; and Norwegian Multicenter Study, 1981). These drugs appear to delay, by an average of two hours, the onset of ventricular fibrillation after symptoms have begun. In that extra two hours, many more patients have arrived in an emergency room.

In regard to the medical management of stress, exercise therapy appears to be efficacious, although there is no evidence to suggest it prolongs life. Patients feel better, sleep better. Exercise improves the quality of life, increases work capacity, and enhances the handling of emotional stress. Doctor James Lynch (1977) has demonstrated that lack of companionship is one of the leading causes of premature death. Death rates are higher in single, widowed, separated, or divorced persons, than in married persons, age-matched for disease and risk factors. There is not only increased death from cardiovascular disease, but all other major causes of death take a higher toll in unmarried persons.

Insurance company statistics have demonstrated that divorced males have a two to six times higher death rate from every major cause of death than married males (DeJong,1978). This includes death from cancer. Social isolation appears to take its greatest risk and toll in coronary disease. Personal rejection makes it more difficult to deal with life stresses. Stronger family associations and extended family support would seem to be helpful. Single persons living alone have a higher incidence of death from heart disease and cancer than their age-matched controls with a stable, extended family environment.

The medical management of stress always, of course, leads to a discussion of hypertension. To be sure, control of blood pressure decreases the incidence of sudden death, as well as decreasing stroke, renal disease, and heart failure. Most patients with hypertension do not "feel it." It is asymptomatic. Additionally, it is difficult to predict for the individual patient when he or she will be hypertensive, as studies with the automatic blood pressure cuff have demonstrated. As an example, some stock brokers had high blood pressure during trading hours on the stock exchange and normal pressure at other times; still other brokers demonstrated high blood pressure at other times, but were normal during the stock exchange trading hours. While the relaxation response elicits a small drop in blood pressure, *drug therapy* for hypertension *is required* and is the mainstay of treatment.

In view of the role of platelets in stress-induced sudden death and acute myocardial infarction, the use of anti-platelet agents, while not managing the stress, can alleviate the consequences of stress-induced platelet change. The use of aspirin and Anturane in this setting appears to be somewhat efficacious and continues under intensive study (Anturane Reinfarction, 1978).

Psychologic support to discontinue cigarette smoking plays a great role in the prevention of sudden death. Additionally, psychologic support to attain and hold the gains from a weight-losing program are also beneficial.

Dr. Eliot emphasizes the use of appropriate leisure time in the medical management of stress (1979). Leisure time needs to be appropriately planned, not the "we have seen it" type of family trip where one returns from the vacation needing a vacation.

In regard to Type A and Type B behavior, it appears that *failing* at Type A is the risk factor rather than *being* Type A per se. Studies by Dembroski (1979) demonstrated that, during an American History quiz, there was an increase in systolic blood pressure in Type B coronary patients—those who had suffered myocardial infarction—but not in Type B controls. Looking further, there is a suggestion that the Type A individuals were better prepared in the subject matter, "more relaxed" in their knowledge of the subject, more confident and, thereby, less stressed by the American History quiz. Thus, it is not simply a matter of Type A, Type B; it is one's perception and *use of Type A* that appears to make the difference. In other words, a Type A individual who reaches his or her goals, appears *not* to have the increased risk.

Blumenthal et al (1980) demonstrated a reduction in the coronary risk profile of a group of Type A men as a result of a structured exercise program. There was also a subsequent decrease in Type A scores.

A general approach to the medical management of stress includes breaking the cycle of more smoking, increased alcohol intake, more overeating, lack of time to exercise, more Valium, more hypnotics for sleep, and on and on.

The use of various transcendental meditation techniques, yoga, biofeedback, and psychotherapy may be useful; less alcohol, caffeine, and nicotine decreases the stress cycle, will decrease PVCs, and will reinforce a calmer emotional state.

Those with residual malignant PVCs, persistent despite elimination of alcohol, nicotine, and caffeine, will require anti-arrhythmic drug therapy. Treating the neurophysiologic trigger would appear to be the more logical approach. Indeed, in studies of patients with sleep-related malignant arrhythmias, documented on Holter Monitoring in their home, merely bringing the patient into the hospital's sleep lab led to a fourfold *decrease* in the number and malignancy of PVCs. The use of hypnotics, particularly barbituates, to suppress REM-sleep-related arrhythmias is particularly dangerous. Sudden cessation of the hypnotic leads to profound REM rebound and more severe ventricular arrhythmias (Shappell & Orr, 1975).

Rapkin(1980) demonstrated that, in men with no prior clinical evidence of ischemic heart disease, sudden cardiac death occurs more often on Mondays than any other day of the week. Men with known cardiac disease experience sudden death uniformly throughout the week.

Similar research, with further investigation into the neurophysiologic triggering events of sudden death, will no doubt lead to increasingly effective management of stress and its consequences.

REFERENCES

Ahlmark, G. et al. Reduction of sudden deaths after myocardial infarction. *Lancet*, 1974, 2, 1563.

Anturane Reinfarction Trial Research Group: Sulfinpyrazone in the prevention of cardiac death after myocardial infarction. *New England Journal of Medicine*, 1978, 298, 289–295.

Baum, R.S. et al. Survival after resuscitation from out-of-hospital ventricular fibrillation. *Circulation*, 1974, *50*, 1231–1235.

Benson, H. Systemic hypertension and the relaxation response. *New England Journal of Medicine*, 1977, *296*, 1152–1156.

Benson, H. Kotch, J.B., Crassweller, K.D., & Greenwood, M.M. Historical and clinical considerations of the relaxation response. *American Scientist*, July-August 1977, *65*. (No.4).

Blumenthal, J.A., Williams, R.S., Williams R.B., et al. Effects of exercise on the type A (coronary prone) behavior pattern. *Psychosomatic Medicine*, 1980, *42*, 289–296.

Buell, J.C., & Eliot, R.S. The clinical and pathological syndromes of sudden cardiac death: An overview. in press.

Cannon, W.B. "Voodoo" death. *Psychosomatic Medicine*, 1957, *19*. 182–190.

Cobb, L.A., Baum, R.S., Alvarez, H, & Schaffer, W.A.. Resuscitation from out-of-hospital ventricular fibrillation. 4 year follow-up. *Circulation*, 1975, 51, 52, Suppl. III: III 223–228.

De Jong, R.H. Hazards of being single. *Journal of the American Medical Association* 1978, *239*, 1533.

Dembroski, T.M., Dougall, J.M., & Lushene, R. Interpersonal interaction and cardiovascular response in type A subjects and coronary patients. *Journal of Human Stress*, 1979, *5*, 28–31.

Eliot, R.S. *Stress and the heart*. Mt. Kisco, N.Y: Futura Publishing Co., 1974.

Eliot, R.S., Clayton, F.C., Pieper, G.M., & Todd, G.L. Influence of environmental stress on the pathogenesis of sudden cardiac death. *Federation Proceedings*, 1977, *36*, 1719–1724.

Eliot, R.S. *Stress and the major cardiovascular disorders*. Mt Kisco, N.Y: Futura Publishing Co., 1979.

Eliot, R.S., Todd, G.L., Clayton, F.C., & Pieper, G.M. Experimental catecholamine-induced acute myocardial necrosis. In V. Manninen & P.I. Jalonen (Eds.), *Sudden coronary death, advances in cardiology*, (Vol. 24). Basel: S. Karger AG, 1978, pp.107–118.

Engel, G.L. Sudden and rapid death during psychological stress. Folklore or folk wisdom. *Annals of Internal Medicine*, 1971, *74*, 771–782.

Engel, G.L. Psychologic factors in instantaneous cardiac death. *New England Journal of Medicine*, 1976, *294*, 664–665.

Engel, G.L. Psychologic stress, vasodepressor (vasovagal) syncope, and sudden death. *Annals of Internal Medicine*, 1978, *89*, 403–412.

Kuller, L., Lilienfeld, A., & Fisher, R.. Epidemiological study of sudden death and unexpected deaths due to atherosclerotic heart disease. *Circulation*, 1966, *34*, 1056–1068.

Lown, B., DeSilva, R.A., & Lenson, R. Role of psychologic stress and autonomic nervous system changes in provocation of ventricular premature complexes. *American Journal of Cardiology*, 1978, 41, 979–985.

Lynch, J.J. *The broken heart*. New York: Basic Books, 1977.

Multicenter International Study: Improvement in prognosis of myocardial infarction by long term beta-adreno receptor blockade using practolol. *Brit Medical Journal*, 1975, *27*, 735–740.

Myers, A., & Dewar, H.A. Circumstances attending 100 sudden deaths from coronary artery disease with coroner's necropsies. *British Heart Journal*, 1975, *37*, 1133–1143.

Norwegian Multicenter Study Group: Timolol-induced reduction in mortality and reinfarction in patients surviving acute myocardial infarction. *New England Journal of Medicine*, 1981, *304*, 801–807.

Rahe, R.H., Romo, M., Bennett, L., & Siltanen, P. Recent life changes, myocardial infarction and abrupt coronary death. *Archives of Internal Medicine*, 1974, *133*, 221–228.

Rahe, R.H., Bennett, L., Romo, M., Siltanen, P., & Arthur, R.J. Subjects recent life changes and coronary heart disease in Finland. *American Journal of Psychiatry*, 1973, *130*, 1222–1224.

Rapkin, S.W.. Chronobiology of cardiac sudden death in men. *Journal of the American Medical Association*, 1980, *244*, 1357–1358.

Schaffer, W.A. et al. Recurrent ventricular fibrillation in modes of death and survivors of out-of-hospital ventricular fibrillation. *New England Journal of Medicine*, 1975, *293*, 259–262.

Shappell, S.D., Orr, W., & Gunn, C.G. The ballooning posterior leaflet syndrome: Minnesota multiphasic personality inventory profiles in symptomatic and asymptomatic groups. *Chest*, 1974, *66*, 690–692.

Shappell, S.D., & Orr, W.C. Variant angina and sleep: A case report with therapeutic considerations. *Diseases of the Nervous System*, 1975, *36*, 295–298.

Simon, A.B. Alonzo, A.A. et al. Sudden death in nonhospitalized cardiac patients: An epidemiological study with implications for intervention techniques. *Archives of Internal Medicine*, 1973, *132*, 163–170.

DISCUSSION

The medical view of stress, chaired by Dr. Shappell, was discussed by: Vincent Gallagher, M.D., Medical Department, Grumman Aerospace Corporation; Maurice Goldenhar, M.D., Associate Professor of Family Medicine, School of Medicine, State University of New York at Stony Brook; Gottfried F. H. Lehmann, M.D., M.A., Medical Director and Chief Medical Officer, Long Island Rail Road; Albert T. Lojko, M.D., New York Area Medical Director, Trans World Airlines; and Julian H. Schwartz, M.D., Consultant in Internal Medicine, South Oaks Hospital.

Dr. Goldenhar:
After 22 years in private practice, I was asked to join the State University faculty in the Department of Family Medicine, mainly to educate physicians to become *family* physicians. We hope to accomplish some of the ideas that may come out of this conference—namely, the reduction of stress, thereby reducing illness. The process includes three years of training following medical school. We now have five affiliated residencies on Long Island, with 77 physicians in training. An important part of the training consists in pointing out the importance of stress in degenerative and other diseases. We think we are on the right track. We think we are able to show these young people that some diseases are naturally the result of infections as well as other processes, as Dr. Shappell pointed out, but may be aggravated by stress. We want to point out that when a patient comes in complaining of a headache or a backache or another such problem, the investigation should not be restricted to those presenting symptoms. It should include a review of all the problems the

individual has experienced during the weeks or months prior to the onset of the chief complaint.

Dr. Schwartz:

I am an internist with a private practice and am also a consultant in medicine at this hospital. In my office, I see a great many people with a variety of complaints, and it is striking that many of the various illnesses may be directly related to stress. We are talking about cardiac illnesses, as Dr. Shappell pointed out—ulcers, colitis, all sorts of problems related to headaches, and many other pyschosomatic illnesses. As a consultant here at South Oaks Hospital, I often see the other end of the spectrum; patients who have had such severe stress that they require psychiatric hospitalization. We often see a very strong tie-in with physical complaints which have been adversely affected by this stress, so I have the perspective of seeing both types of patients, and often what I learn from one will help me with another.

Dr. Lojko:

My background is twofold. I was in private practice for four years, during which time I became a Valium distributor. Recently I became Medical Director of Trans World Airlines here in New York. It is our philosophy that there is, indeed, stress in the workplace and it does affect employees' productivity. We hope that it affects productivity in a positive way, but we are aware that at times stress does affect productivity adversely. In the airline industry, we have additional factors that contribute to stress—shift work, traveling across datelines, traveling across different time zones, commuting long distances before beginning work. We generally believe that the stress demonstrated by the employee is in the realm of behavioral medical disorders and is frequently reflected in alcoholism, drug abuse, a mental health problem, or an inability to adapt to situations. We believe that stress relates to an employee's job, but we don't, as a premise, accept that the workplace itself is the cause of these problems.

At TWA, we have an Employee Assistance Program with a full-time coordinator, myself, another physician, and a physician's assistant. We have an open-door policy and attempt in every way possible to communicate to our union members as well as our employees that we want to assist them with their personal problems, which they may be bringing to the workplace, and with any other stresses which may be adversly affecting their work. In that way we can direct them to the necessary psychiatric or psychological help.

Dr. Gallagher:

We have been seeing a growing incidence of cardiovascular disease among 45 to 55 year olds. We obviously don't know all the reasons. But I think one reason is directly related to stress. These men have one or two children in college, their wives are now employed outside the home, they hold a second and sometimes a third job. How can they be productive when they're working all these jobs? I frankly don't know. Also, because Grumman Aerospace Corporation is worldwide, we have approximately 400 to 600 employees who are on board navy ships and out at sea for long periods. These men are separated from their families for six to nine months at a time, with no emotional support, and that creates problems.

Dr. Lehmann:

As the Medical Director of the Long Island Rail Road (LIRR), I am aware not only of employee stress, but also of the stresses of 250,000 daily commuters who have or encounter problems on their way to and from work.

As a matter of background, I am board-certified in Family Practice, and also in Industrial Medicine. I have a master's degree in education (Human Relations) and I taught high school in New York City for a year. I had extensive working experience before I became a doctor. To give you examples, I worked for two-and-a-half years as an air traffic controller, for two years in a bank, and for three years for the telephone company. I did this while working my way through college and university. I even worked for a while as a trainman for a railroad in South Australia. So, I am familiar with a variety of jobs and requirements, which is very helpful in making decisions affecting job performance.

On the LIRR we have an alcoholism program which is served

by three full-time counselors, one of whom is close to his Ph.D. We have expanded this program recently to include drug addiction and family counseling. Despite our emphasis we are really quite limited, because we don't have enough counselors for our 7,000 employees. To provide services of this kind is a tremendous undertaking.

Dr. Shappell:

We have heard several definitions of stress, but the one I like best is the lack of personal options: feeling trapped, feeling that one has no control over one's current situation. Studies on life change units have high on their list: death of a spouse, divorce, etc., but is is *prolonged* stress that causes trouble, prolonged stress for which there is no easy solution. It is the sense of being trapped, unable to cope. If one's daughter or son is picked up with heroin, this is a prolonged stress. Nothing you can do makes it go away. It works on you week after week. Prolonged stress can lead, in certain situations, to sudden death or illness. But certainly we know that not all stress is bad. Stress has been likened to a violin string. If the string is pulled too tightly, it snaps; if it is too loose, it doesn't make music. The proper amount of stress is needed for human performance.

Audience:

Dr. Lojko, when there is a plane crash, do you find that the stress on your personnel works in a positive way, that they become more careful?

Dr. Lojko:

I think you get a two-pronged effect in terms of stress. The cockpit crew doesn't have the kind of stress from flying that you or I have; they're almost more comfortable there than anyone else. The other crew members are constantly trained in the attitude of safety and have a sense of confidence. Initially, when an accident happens, the stressful situation is non-productive. It becomes anxiety producing—I knew somebody on that plane, or I flew out of that area two weeks ago. It has a negative effect. Subsequent to the shock of the incident, the adaptive mechanisms take over and they begin to say, well, I had better be prepared. It becomes a positive stressful reaction. I have to qualify that, because it depends on each individual. Some people are not as comfortable with flying as the crew is. Occasionally you will get a negative effect which is not countered by a positive one. Usually, however, the reaction is transient, maybe a month or two.

Audience:

Studies in Belfast and in Britain, comparing home program patients treated for acute infarcts versus those in the hospital, show evidence that the death rate is less at home than in the hospital.

Dr. Shappell:

The problem with the studies is two-fold. One is that the physicians or attendants decide who is sicker, so the sicker people go to the hospital. Secondly, as my British colleagues tell me, the study is totally invalid, but the government is pushing it as valid because they, in fact, don't have the facilities to treat people in the intensive care setting. It has become a political issue rather than just a medical one.

Audience:

How does denying one's heart disease affect the outcome of the disease?

Dr. Shappell:

Those who suffer a heart attack, who are hospitalized, sent home, and who deny their illness, do best—provided cessation of smoking and taking one's medicine is not ignored.

Audience:

What is some of the evidence for stress-induced sudden death?

Dr. Shappell:

Animals who are made familiar with all the lab personnel almost never have a cardiac arrest from ventricular fibrillation secondary to induced myocardial infarct. Whereas, if you take animals from the same litters and suddenly bring them into the lab and a heart attack is induced, something like 40 percent of them go into ventricular fibrillation. In addition, one of the reasons morphine is particularly effective in the early stages of heart attack treatment is because it not only relieves the pain, but in animal studies it tends to prevent ventricular fibrillation. That is, it tends to prevent the heart stopping, and the central nervous system is altered by the morphine. One's perception of one's disease is altered, and survival is greater.

Dr. Goldenhar:

Speaking of coronary care units, a doctor I know was admitted to a coronary care unit where he received the best of care and had no complications. On the fifth day when he was ready for discharge to a cardiology floor, he then became extremely stressed because he didn't want to leave the unit. He felt a greater sense of security there.

Dr. Schwartz:

I think much depends on the design of the coronary care unit. The designs of these units have evolved greatly since they first started. When I was in training, our first coronary unit was crowded, with a lot of patients close to one another, and a great deal of hustle and bustle going on. When a severe medical problem or a medical catastrophe like a cardiac arrest occurred with one of the patients, of course it had a very adverse effect on the other patients. Since that time, the coronary units are being redesigned to give each patient more privacy, although I must say they could be further developed. A well-designed unit would eliminate much anxiety and pressure.

Audience:

I believe that more liberal visiting hours in the intensive setting would be beneficial. Family and friends can often bring great moral support.

Dr. Shappell:

It depends on who is visiting. For example, when you monitor rhythms, if there is a divorce pending and the spouse visits, there are increased arrhythmias. It is interesting, too, that when you try to separate out adrenalin or sympathetic versus parasympathetic effects, you find that when a business partner with whom there has been some problem comes to visit, there is an increase in the heart rate. When a spouse comes in, there are PVC's. In other words, it is not the same. You can't sit there and predict, given there will be trouble, what that individual's reaction will be to the trouble. Some of it will trigger ventricular arrhythmias, others will increase sinus rate, others will slow profoundly. All of these are stress reactions. You cannot accurately predict what will happen. Why do certain kinds of stressful situations or discussions precipitate certain reactions? Futhermore, when you look at people in coronary care units, invariably the life stress unit totals have gone up, and so when you consider visitors, you must think of the source of all those stresses. Simply opening the doors may make for more, rather than fewer, problems.

Audience:

We mostly accept that stress affects productivity. Do your companies have a positive program to help the employee understand stress while trying to increase productivity?

Dr. Gallagher:

At Grumman we have various programs. I think our most important program is nursing stations in most of our major manufacturing plants. These stations are staffed with trained registered nurses. At any time, any employee can go into any one of these nursing stations for consultation. With the first perception of the problem, the individual has an almost instantaneous outlet. As a backup, we work over in central medical headquarters; if there is a question the nurse will call us. If the nurse perceives that the situation calls for the employee talking with one of the doctors, we arrange for that.

Audience:

You don't really have a program to help them understand stress. They have to know they have a severe problem before they come to you for help. Do you have any preventive education?

Dr. Gallagher:

We do at the nursing stations, as well as at the central medical department. Literature is given to the employee, and if the employee comes in, the nurse will then go through the literature and try to resolve the problems. But we do not reach out in a preventive manner.

Dr. Lojko:

To answer your question pertaining to Trans World Airlines specifically, do we have an educational stress-oriented program that meets at such and such a time? No. Are we positively and aggressively attacking stressful situations that may affect our peoples' performance? I think we are in the best way we can under the circumstances. You have to understand the environment in which we are working. We are dealing with unions which, at times, are reticent about telling us their problems. However, we have frequent meetings with both the International Association of Machinists (IAM) and the Airline Pilots Association, and we actively seek out their counsel. Where are your problems? Where can we help you? Do you have developing situations?

We do have monthly monitoring meetings with the Airline Pilots Association's especially-appointed representatives, the flight operations people, and the medical department people. These meetings and conferences are confidential. We have three medical departments and six physicians located throughout the country. Each section has a full-time Special Health Services coordinator. They know about treatment programs and it is part of their responsibility to search out these programs. But, again, like Grumman, we have the problem—how do you get the employees to come during their time off? They are not too interested unless there is a crisis. When we hear there is a problem, we ask them to tell us and we will help. We have personnel who are willing to help.

Dr. Lehmann:

Our employees are dispersed throughout Long Island and New York City. We have one centralized medical department, and we have access to the various hospitals and emergency rooms throughout Long Island and New York City. We do not have a stress prevention program per se. We are limited in what we are allowed to do for our employees because of binding contracts and rules and regulations which are laid down at negotiation time. We have 17 different unions. We are not allowed to transfer an employee under stress to a different job. That would get everybody very upset.

We have railroad police officers who say that after 17 years on the force they are afraid to touch a gun; they are afraid to get involved in an argument or to make an arrest where unwillingly they might have to resort to the use of a gun, and they do not want to continue to work under those pressurized circumstances. However, we cannot transfer them somewhere else. This takes negotiation — dealing and haggling about rights, preferences, and priorities — which often becomes a time problem; sometimes employees are away from their jobs for years before the representative union and management, together with another union who will bargain for a particular employee, will agree on placing this employee into a different job category.

We have problems with engineers who are afraid to continue operating a train. We must take them out of service and disqualify them for their job. If they do not have sufficient seniority, the Railroad Retirement Board does not accept their disability, and the employee may have to look for a job somewhere else after all that time on the railroad. That's because of contract regulations concerning transfer into a different job.

There are certain stresses we *are* dealing with. These include aspects of alcoholism. If the employee has been identified as an alcoholic or is en route to becoming an alcoholic to the extent that it affects his work performance, we *must* intercede and refer him to a counselor. The employee *must* adhere to the guidelines laid down by the counselor. If an employee has problems that he is afraid to bring to the supervisor's attention, he has the right to get in touch with a counselor without bringing in the medical department. The counselor may advise him or arrange for him to go to an outside group.

We are now trying to get involved in family counseling. However, our efforts without extensive staffing must remain limited, because there are many priority problems. Our main priority is to keep the trains running—that consumes most of the money. To start family counseling we would need vast amounts of money and a large staff. Right now we have only three full-time counselors, and if we want our family counseling to have impact, besides more staff we must have more cooperation from the unions, more cooperation from management, and more cooperation from the employees. Money will have to be approved by the Metropolitan Transit Authority for just that purpose. There are many ramifications.

Dr. Goldenhar:

May I point out what the American Academy of Family Physicians and the Society of Teachers of Family Medicine have done? They have mounted a program to help recognize those residents in training who may become impaired. This permits us to "rescue" these physicians. Courses on prevention are offered at various meetings of these organizations.

Dr. Shappell:

The stress on the job or the job loss of your patients, your employees, or your colleagues is accompanied by a significant increase in their life-change-unit total. Your advice to them should be that this is not the setting or time to do five other things. When there is job loss, or marital difficulty, or loss of a spouse, one does not take on more debt or increase life stress units, because as the totals increase in areas in which the individual has no control, he has to drop out in other areas to compensate.

Audience:

Corporations might consider including a stress management program in the initial training program, because stress seems to have become part of all job descriptions. You wouldn't have to take employees off the job or ask them to come in during their lunch hour or after hours—which, in fact, may be an additional stress—if you prepared them *before* the problem occurs. Do you think the unions would object to this proposal?

Dr. Lehmann:

If the issue is politically advantageous to the unions, they will go for it. If they feel that the issue infringes upon their rights, they will be against it. The same applies to management. Don't forget, we haven't even considered the willingness or readiness of the employee.

Dr. Lojko:

I appreciate your thoughts, but we are dealing in the real world with people who do not fully appreciate the definition of stress. We don't encourage commuting from California to New York to fly to Greece, all in one day. Some of our work rules imply that. But, remember, we are talking about stress as it develops, and changeable factors which suddenly come upon a person. He doesn't understand it at age 22; he may get the stress at 33, because, by that time he has a family, children, and life's not so good because his kid was arrested for smoking pot. Once or twice a year we go out with our special services coordinators to talk to managers at different airport facilities to re-emphasize to them that we are interested in helping anyone showing symptoms of stress.

Audience:

What is the first step in relieving personal stress?

Dr. Shappell:

The biggest coping skill involves defining; having each individual realize what his stress level is, and then identifying specific areas where he can lower the totals. The problems that lead to disease are *chronic* stress issues. An irony of chronic stress is that often the danger comes with the sudden *release* of the chronic stress. For example, an individual in the midst of several complicated situations, who keeps saying, well, let's just wait until this is done and then, until something else is done, seems to be doing all right. However, the danger—at least from the standpoint of sudden death—is in the phase of sudden release. After long, complicated divorce proceedings, the individual who is prone, dies a sudden death the day *after* the divorce has been settled. Or the father who has been preparing for his daughter's wedding is fine up to the wedding, but he dies the next night. Studies of sudden death show that 75 percent of the people who die sudden deaths die at home. A traveling businessman, for example, who has been on the road for three weeks, comes home and says, am I glad that is over with, and sits down and dies. In other words, it is prolonged stress with a sudden release that causes a neural confusion between the adrenalin system that was predominantly operating during the trip and the parasympathetic system trying to take over.

Dr. Schwartz:

Now that stress is increasingly recognized, it would seem to me that a specialized worker could be trained to make the rounds in a company or plant to evaluate, and spot stresses that can be corrected. A simple thing like a dirty bathroom can be stressful. That specialized "stress spotter" could visit each department, speak to employees, ask them questions about where they feel stress is a problem, inspect the working conditions, and so forth. They would then give recommendations to management.

Dr. Shappell:

In industry, and in all of life, everyone needs a strong sense that someone cares, that there is someone to turn to. One of the problems with people who live alone, and their numbers are increasing enormously in this country, is that they lose a major coping mechanism. There is no one to turn to, to say, help me through this crisis. Interestingly, many of the studies show that the helping person does not have to be a physician or a psychiatrist; that person could be a good friend, a minister, a priest, rabbi. Someone has to be around who genuinely cares and is there. That is a major coping mechanism that industry can make available.

Audience:

I am a psychotherapist in private practice and I am a consultant for employee assistance programs. There have been two points made that I would like to pick up on. One is that stress is a constant that we have to learn to live with, and the second is that unfulfilled expectations create additional stress which can at some point become distress. As a physician, either in industry or in private practice, patients come to you with a certain set of expectations. Oftentimes they want a cure for a set of symptoms or an illness that they are struggling with, and when it relates to stress-related difficulties, oftentimes physicians can't give patients cures but can more appropriately help with a set of controls or a regimen of behaviors that will *help* with control. That puts stress on the physician who is expected to cure but does not have the tools to cure stress-related problems. The patient, as a result, has unmet expectations because his or her stress cannot be alleviated with a pill.

How do you, as physicians, deal with the fulfilled and unfulfilled expectations of your patients and the expectations of yourselves as healers when you can't always "heal" stress? How do you make decisions about which patients do best with Valium, and if it is chronic stress, how long ought they to be treated with Valium? Which patients ought to be referred for psychotherapy? And, lastly, since most patients would rather not be viewed as having an emotional or mental problem and do not want to go to a psychotherapist because that implies to them that they are maladaptive or even crazy, how do you work with this kind of distress?

Dr. Lojko:

We are fortunate that each of our medical departments has a computerized EKG, laboratory facilities, chest X-rays—all that any physician could possibly want.

I'll use a hypothetical case. An employee comes in complaining of palpitations, he is going to die, he is sure he is having a heart attack, and he is rushed up. They are giving him oxygen, and then comes the doctor. He is going to save him. We do everything and there is really nothing wrong with him. We do a urinalysis, it's normal. The blood work is normal. The guy is sure he is going to die, yet his EKG says he couldn't be more normal than if he were a newborn. We listen carefully to him, which is very important. A physician does his physical. We don't tell a nurse to tell us what she thinks and have her bring him into our office. We physically go there as if he were a private patient. Subsequently, we bring him in and show him that the test results are normal.

Meanwhile, while we are doing the workup, I have already notified the special health services coordinator, saying, stand by, I think I am going to need you. Then we explain what we have done in a logical step-by-step way. As the individual calms down, we try to delve. "What happened this morning?" "How are things at home?" "Are your kids in trouble?" "Was your boss on your back?"

While he is getting worked up, we will frequently contact the union and ask if they know anything about possible problems. We call the supervisor and ask, "Do you know anything?" Often we hear, "Well, he has been acting funny", or "We thought he had a problem", or "He has been sick a few days", or "His wife is sick." If he is not willing to volunteer information in the privacy of the doctor's office, we kind of nudge him with questions.

Once he begins to understand what is going on, I try to explain to him that there is really nothing physically wrong with you, but at this point you don't have the mechanisms necessary to cope with all the difficulties you had earlier this morning. You don't have the mechanisms—not because you didn't try to learn them, not because you were not taught them, not because you are stupid—but because you are overwhelmed. It is like trying to make an engine do 110 rpm's, when it is designed for only 100.

We try not to encourage the use of any drugs. We feel we do better in a drug-free environment. Obviously, being in aviation medicine, we don't like to think that anybody working on the planes, flying the planes, or responsible for safety would need a drug to get through the day. So we continue to talk to see how best we can help. Sometimes I say, why don't you come back tomorrow and we'll do another EKG in case we missed something. To reassure him, I'll show him another normal EKG. That serves two purposes: it double-protects us and it encourages him. Another thing we might do is speak to a shop steward or to a manager, and say, "Look, we're here, we're open, tell him to come back if he wants to."

Dr. Gallagher:

We are not dispensers of Valium or other medications. With such an individual, we would attempt to assess the situation when he comes in. If it seems to be a psychologic disorder, after screening we talk with the individual and point him in the direction of either his family doctor for further consultation, or to the good backup in psychotherapy that we have here at South Oaks. For the most part we get him pointed in the right direction.

Dr. Goldenhar:

In our training of young physicians, we emphasize team effort, and our social workers offer the kind of counseling we would like the patient to have.

Dr. Lehmann:

Some stresses cannot be changed: one has to meet deadlines, one has to fly planes at a certain time, one has to run trains at a certain time. If people are under stress because of having to meet deadlines and cannot do anything about those deadlines, they have to *learn* to deal with those stresses. Some people can cope better than others. People who cannot cope with stress are the ones who come to us with illness, e.g., chest pains, headaches, back pains, and so on. They don't know why they feel sick, because they don't realize that stress on the job or at home is causing the symptoms. If you work in a factory on an assembly line, you are also under stress. You cannot modify that stress, the work has to be done.

Ideally, if a "non-working" patient comes to the office with certain stress symptoms, the doctor can tell him, "Look; modify your stress, move away, or get involved with other kinds of people; talk to the priest or rabbi or counselor." I don't think dealing with stress can be taught, but you can be taught how to cope with problems by either modifying your own behavior or modifying the stress itself.

Dr. Shappell:

People can be made more aware of their actions. Few people really sit down and think about what they are doing in a total life setting. As an example, somebody who is 45 who has had his first heart attack tells me he is buying a bigger house. I talk very specifically to him. Why do you need a bigger house in a better neighborhood now? Why do you need a bigger car? Why put yourself under such financial stress? I tell him, in this situation, you have to cut down. He will say, gee, I can't; I have a new wife, some additional children and I am in a rising phase of obligations. I say, well, you have to get yourself in a position where you can cut down. *That* is an individual who feels trapped. Several people like that have died sudden death. So, if one sits and talks, I think one can catch a patient or an employee in this general discussion by saying, look at all of these life stresses, look at all of these totals; perhaps you don't realize it, but this is *specific* advice, not general advice. So I think one can cope by *not* getting into certain situations.

Audience:

I teach coping and coping strategy to young people, and this is where I think it belongs. If you get young people in your place of work to understand what some stresses are and what they do, that might be a start.

Dr. Lehmann:

You cannot force people to change their behavior. It has to be voluntary. There has to be insight and motivation. A lot of people are not interested in changing their lifestyles, despite all the stress they have. You remove those stresses and they are miserable. We are making efforts, as I pointed out, to get our employees involved in counseling programs. The posters which we place around the property are usually removed overnight by employees. We still have difficulties with our alcohol program, despite its beneficial existence for many years. Employees feel we are infringing on their personal lives. They do not always have the proper insight to realize that what they do on the outside, as far as alcohol and drugs are concerned, does affect their working performance, and if it does affect their working performance, we do have the right to intercede. But, what I want to point out is that employees—whether they be workers, union people, managers, or top executives—have not been trained to have a medical view of these problems, and we cannot re-educate them.

Dr. Shappell:

An important consideration, in regard to an individual's responsiveness to education in coping mechanisms, relates to educational level. Specific studies demonstrate that sudden death and stress-related sudden death are a phenomenon of greater intensity in lower educational levels. The greater one's educational level is, the less frequent is the phenomenon of sudden death. Now, why is that? A small degree can be attributed to smoking as a major risk factor. That is to say, the greater one's education, the more one actually believes the mass of data that smoking is harmful, and the more one has the will to act on it. But even subtracting such elements, it appears as though the more stress factors a person is aware of, the better his coping mechanisms are organized to deal with issues.

Audience:

We hear that stress can cause sudden death. Is there any drug remedy that will give the same kind of dramatic relief from stress as penicillin does from pneumococcal pneumonia?

Dr. Shappell:

There is nothing available now. However, with the discovery of many neurotransmitters in the central nervous system, and with the studies on lithium for manic depressives, it is clear that an individual's reactions to stress and perhaps other psychiatric illnesses may ultimately have some biochemical basis. When those reactions are more clearly defined, and interfering or blocking agents are designed, we may have a more specific therapy to

counteract or prevent the sensation of stress with its consequences. But that is still a while off.

Audience:

The emphasis has been on the worker, and how to relieve
his stress. Are there programs for management? If the personal
relationships between management and worker were improved,
perhaps that would help in the overall program to relieve stressful situations.

Dr. Gallagher:

I think that is beyond the medical field and more in the
administrative and personnel management fields. When I talk
about workers, I include the chairman of the board right down
to the sweeper. Grumman's open door policy is open door for
anyone. That means top management, middle management,
shop people, etc. When I speak about the worker it crosses all
sections.

Yes, stress is found in upper management as well as middle
management. There is stress for the maintenance person who,
with respect to "equal opportunity," has been told he is being
discriminated against, because he has not been given an opportunity to advance himself. So he comes in and says, "I don't want
to do anything different, I like my job, I don't want to change
my job, there is nothing else I want to do." Who has put stress
on this man? Not the company, not the individual, but people
who insist on "equal opportunity" whether the person wants it
or not.

Dr. Lojko:

I would echo the same thing. When I talk about employees,
I talk about *all* of them.

Dr. Lehmann:

Workers include everybody from the top to the bottom and
from the bottom to the top. Everybody has the same right—equal
access to all medical services—and we give freely with all good

intent. We do have a different situation with management; as management is not unionized, there are certain possibilities which do not exist in the rank and file. Management can be transferred sideways: they receive promotions, they receive demotions. And, as you know, both successes and failures are associated with stress. There can be tremendous stresses which result in tremendous symptomatology.

Managers, as a group, are more educated than workers. This doesn't mean that management makes more money than the worker. We have some workers such as baggagemen, car maintenance people, station cleaners, who can earn $30,000 a year, with overtime. This salary range gives them a degree of freedom that can make up for frustrations on the job. Management does not make as much money, as far as I know. Management doesn't get overtime pay. They may have to work a seven-day week and get compensatory time off. If there is an emergency, they have to come in to work, whether they have outside commitments or not. The job has to be done.

Managers, as a class, may have a different life style mitigating their stress. It is interesting to note that we have college graduates who are menial workers because they do not want to handle the stress of being management, of making decisions, of being responsible for the performance of others. We all know other people often don't do what they are told to do. Ninety-two percent of the stress on executives is from subordinates not doing their job properly. Well, in a situation like that, you, as a manager, may have to force somebody. You don't want or like to do it, but in order to increase productivity or to reduce your own stress, you may have to fire employees. This can become very difficult if the employee is covered by a union contract, because then the manager really can't do his job. He also cannot ask his subordinates to produce more, because the union will get involved and will talk about rights and contracts. We have executives who suffer from ulcers because of these situations. And, of course, our union representatives suffer from the same ailments. There are no easy solutions. We try to deal with them as we can, and sometimes we successfully use one method with one person, while the same method fails with someone else.

Audience:

Could you tell us a little bit about the Type A and the Type B personalities in regard to the current thinking on cardiovascular disease and its relation to the work environment?

Dr. Shappell:

Good question to raise. The Type A personality is an aggressive, impatient, time-conscious individual who sets out to accomplish many goals. The Type B personality is really the opposite. But the problem comes if one is typed as an "A" and fails at Type A; that is, when the individual sets out goals, but never seems to be happy even when the goals are attained. The individual sets more goals and never quite reaches any degree or level of satisfaction. So a Type A can be subgrouped. Simply comparing the Type A with the Type B, without other provisions, does not make a very strong distinction between them. As I had mentioned this morning, studies used to compare Type A and Type B, such as blood pressure during exams, are objective stress indicators. The Type B can have as high a blood pressure as the Type A. Finally, we must consider the strength of risk factors. There is a major difference between Type A and the so-called coronary-prone personality. So, there continues to be debate as to whether the Type A/Type B makes a difference in terms of the development of heart disease, and how strong the risk factor is.

When one looks at risk factors, you must consider the *overall* risk. For example, a recent study on pancreatic cancer showed that coffee drinkers had a doubled risk of developing pancreatic cancer. Well, that's true, but if you consider the overall risk of pancreatic cancer, doubling it would still not put anyone in a threatened category. It may be rather dramatic to say the risk is doubled, but one has to determine the numerator and denominator. There are plenty of Type A's who attend the funerals of their Type B compatriots. Thus, there has to be much more study. There is no question that typing personalities serves to define broad categories of personality and the influence of stress.

Dr. Goldenhar:

To accent what Dr. Shappell said, there are some people who may well represent the Type A and some who represent the Type B, but most of us, I am certain, are in between; we are partly "A" and partly "B".

Audience:

Is there any difference in the perception of stress in the two personality types?

Dr. Shappell:

If you take Type A's and divide them into coronary-prone and non-coronary-prone groups, you will find the coronary-prone individual is the one who perceives all sorts of issues and goals as stressful. The non-coronary-prone Type A can more easily move from one goal to the next.

Dr. Lehmann:

I believe I can summarize: if you like your job, you live longer.

INDEX

Absenteeism, 60, 104
Adaptation to Life (George Vaillant), 114
Adolescence and stress, 46–47, 125
Affirmative Action programs, 72–73
Alcoholism, 60, 74, 95, 99, 124, 130–131, 154, 155, 161
Allport, Gordon, 126
Anatomy of an Illness (Norman Cousins), 127
Anxiety, as part of stress, 128

Behavior Medicine Society, The, 116
Biofeedback, 23, 125, 150
Blue-collar stress, 56–57, 59, 60–64
Boredom as stressor, 32
Burnout, 73, 95

Calcium channel blockers, 147
Cardiovascular disease; *see* Sudden cardiac death
Change as stressor, 12–13, 70, 81, 87–88, 90, 93, 94, 96
Children and stress, 44–47

Chronic stress, 84–85, 156, 163, 165
Coagulative myocytolysis, 146
Communication, 99–101
Control, 20, 35, 120
Coronary care units, 158–159
Counseling, employee, 23, 53–54
Cousins, Norman, 127
Craft of Power, The (Ralph Siu), 4
Crisis intervention, 98
Crisis stress, 84, 164
Cultist panaceas, 89–90

Death, 97–98
Discrimination as source of stress, 33
Distress, 44, 46, 110, 114, 118, 137
Divorce, 60, 122
Drug addiction as response to stress, 31–32, 46, 60, 125, 154
Drugs, mood-altering, 97, 164, 166, 167
Dubos, René, 127

Education, 29, 76–77, 98, 169
Endocrine responses to stress, 17, 60

Ergonomics, 32
Eustress, 114, 115, 118
Executive stress, 105, 107–108
Exercise therapy, 23, 148
Experiential stress, 70–71, 97

Family stress, 44–47, 52–53, 63
  dual-career families, 52–53, 65
Fight-or-flight response, 17, 95, 120
Fromm, Erich (quoted), 2
Future Shock (Alvin Toffler), 81

Hazardous substances in the workplace, 58–59, 60, 69
Health care workers, 16
Health insurance benefits, 62–63, 71–72, 109–110
  mental health coverage, 63, 71–72
Holmes-Rahe scale, 118, 122–123, 138–139
Homosexuals, 89
Humor, 122, 127
Hypertension, 22, 23, 143, 144, 148–149
Hypnosis, 147

Isolation, 102, 148

Jacques, Elliott, 2
Job restructuring, 23, 25, 61

Levinson, Daniel J., 9, 10

Marital states, changes in, 12
  see also Divorce
Master Manager, The (Ralph Siu), 4
Measurement of stress, 47–49
Middle-management stress, 106–107, 170–171
Minorities, 87

Neurotransmitters, 145–146, 147–148, 169–170

Occupational Health and Safety Act (OSHA), 58, 59
Organizational stress, 25–26, 38–39, 49
  measurement of, 49

Participation management, 36, 38, 61–62, 66–67, 73
Productivity
  American workers' versus other countries', 49–50, 136
  Japanese workers', 49, 50–51, 135–136
  and labor unrest, 57
  and management, 54, 129–130, 133–136, 139
  measurement of, 51–52
  and time breaks, 105
Psychiatry, 103–104

Relaxation response, 147
Retirement, 19
Role ambiguity, 20–21, 32, 42
Role conflict, 21
Role reassessment, 86

Seasons of a Man's Life, The (Daniel J. Levinson), 9, 10
Security, job, 19, 63–64, 67
Self-esteem, 96, 102–103, 130
Self-help groups, 90, 95
Seyle, Hans, 113, 114, 116, 120, 129, 132
Seyle's Guide to Stress Research, 114
Shift work, 36–37, 43
Siu, Ralph, 4–5
Social support, 81–82, 91, 93
Stress
  definitions of, 5, 113–114, 120, 123, 128–129, 132, 156
  hypothesis, 123–124, 129
  management programs, 22–27
  prevention of, 40–41
  (see also Chronic stress; Crisis stress; Executive stress; Experiential stress; Family stress; Middle-management stress)
Stressors, 3–9, 12–13, 17, 19–21, 29–30, 115, 129
Sudden cardiac death, 142–150, 157–158, 164, 169

Third Wave, The (Alvin Toffler), 81
Thomas Lewis (quoted), 117
Time sharing, 78

Toffler, Alvin, 81
Tokenism, 86–87
Transcending the Power Game (Ralph Siu), 4
Type A/Type B behavior, 149, 172–173

Unemployment, 68–69

Vaillant, George, 114
Value systems, 34, 106
Vulnerability
    individual, 7–9, 18, 21, 23, 31
    organizational, 25–26

Women workers, 56, 58–59, 65, 74–75, 77–78, 87, 136–137
    (*see also* Family stress: dual-career families)
Women's movement, 86, 88–89
Work
    and community, 21–22
    as coping mechanism, 2
    environment, 20, 29, 35–36, 58–59, 60, 69
    ethic, 105–106
    schedules, 25, 43, 78